My Cricket Companion

My Cricket Companion

Alec Stewart

CORINTHIAN BOOKS

Published in the UK in 2009 by
Corinthian Books, an imprint of
Icon Books Ltd, Omnibus Business Centre,
39–41 North Road, London N7 9DP
email: info@iconbooks.co.uk
www.iconbooks.co.uk

Sold in the UK, Europe, South Africa and Asia
by Faber & Faber Ltd, Bloomsbury House,
74–77 Great Russell Street, London WC1B 3DA

Distributed in the UK, Europe, South Africa and Asia
by TBS Ltd, TBS Distribution Centre, Colchester Road
Frating Green, Colchester CO7 7DW

This edition published in Australia in 2009
by Allen & Unwin Pty Ltd,
PO Box 8500, 83 Alexander Street,
Crows Nest, NSW 2065

Distributed in Canada by
Penguin Books Canada,
90 Eglinton Avenue East, Suite 700,
Toronto, Ontario M4P 2YE

ISBN: 978-190685-000-5

Typeset in New Baskerville by Marie Doherty

Printed and bound in the UK by
CPI Mackays, Chatham ME5 8TD

Contents

Note

Some players discussed or referenced in the book are still active and so associated statistics are correct at time of going to press.

Introduction

Someone asked me recently what the best shot was I ever played in Test cricket. I'm slightly ashamed to say that I was able to answer with absolutely no need for pause of thought whatsoever. I don't suppose it was because the shot was the greatest the game has ever seen, or that it was so special it was discussed in pubs up and down the country that evening. I suppose you will also have to trust me when I tell you that I don't still relentlessly analyse the best and worst moments of my career! There are certain things in life that we all have clarity about and that single moment is one of mine.

That level of clarity cannot, unfortunately, be said of the career choice that led me to that moment. As a teenager I was playing for Wimbledon's youth team and plotting my life out as a professional footballer. One day my coach, Dario Gradi, called me in and said he'd heard I was a good cricketer. It was his way of providing clarity to the situation – and me with a life-defining moment. In more basic terms, it was his way of saying that I would have more chance trying to make the grade as a cricketer!

I obviously took heed and, as much as I love football, have no regrets whatsoever. It is strange, however, to think that a game with a leather ball, a few bits of wood that stick out of the ground and another bit that we swing around the place has defined my life so far. It has taken me around the world several times, from the ground of my club side,

Malden Wanderers (where I've played since the age of six), to the Oval and Lord's, Lilac Hill on the River Swan, the 100,000-strong crowds of Eden Gardens and the MCG, and back again. Of course there have been highs and lows along the way but there is one aspect of it all of which I have absolutely no doubt: cricket is right up there as the best sport in the world.

That's why I've compiled this book. It's allowed me to analyse and celebrate a game that I love. But be warned: there is no real chronological or systematic flow to it all. It is simply a large selection of random thoughts about the game that I still seem to have beyond my playing days: my great memories of the past, and excitement (and cautions) for cricket's future – basically a random mishmash of stats, facts and rants that I've wanted to put together for ages, and now have. Some opinions you might agree with, others you won't, I'm sure. Either way, I hope you enjoy it …

Alec Stewart
May 2009

———————————————————

Oh yeah. In case you wanted to know, it was a hooked Curtly Ambrose bouncer that I saw early at The Oval in 1991. He even clapped it and for a quick like Curtly to do that, perhaps it *was* the best shot that the world has ever seen after all!

"

Cricket is the greatest game that the wit of man has yet devised.

Plum Warner

"

You *can* have too much of a good thing

Whether you like it or not, there is no doubting that Twenty20 has given cricket a great boost. Although always an integral part of club cricket – either as fifteen eight-ball over midweek twilight cricket or just a straight twenty-over game – for some reason it has taken the professional game until now to embrace it. When it was first discussed in 2002, prior to its introduction in 2003, I'll be the first to admit that my reaction – and the reaction in general in the Surrey dressing room at that time – was far from enthusiastic. The prevailing consensus was that it's a slogathon: a gimmick for the professional game, and that we'd just get the youngsters in the club to play.

On 13 June 2003 Surrey played Middlesex at the Oval as one of the first official Twenty20 matches, played for the inaugural Twenty20 Cup. I didn't play but I thought I'd bring my 10-year-old lad and a couple of his mates from school up to watch. As we came down the Clapham Road and got within 400 yards of the ground, I thought that there must have been an accident or an incident of some sort because of the massive crowd that had developed by that entrance of the ground. It turned out my scepticism for the new form of the professional game wasn't shared by the public, as the huge crowds at the gate were trying to get into a near-enough-full ground, for the start of the match.

The public had clearly bought into Twenty20 straight away – sooner than the players really. But your average county player does not get to play in front of 20,000 people too often, unless they're in a Lord's final, and so from that moment, Twenty20 never looked back.

I think it's been absolutely fantastic, given cricket an injection of energy as much as anything, at all levels. Of course there will be the cricket purists, who will always turn their noses up at it, but even they can't deny that it has attracted a whole new audience to the game. Perhaps they might not all be the sort of cricket fan that would happily sit through six and a half hours of play during each day of a regulation four-day county game, or would necessarily appreciate a well-left ball in a Test Match, but if it means there is new interest in the game – in whatever guise – that can only be a good thing.

My only concern – and it is a big concern – is that we don't flood the market with Twenty20. We should work on the basis that if you drip-feed something, people always want more of it. In its first year each county had three home games – people stuck those dates in their diaries and made sure they didn't miss them. If you give people too much of something the novelty value will quickly wear off and they will inevitably want to move on to something else. So I'm wary that, with an increasing number of Twenty20 games scheduled in England year on year, it doesn't get out of hand. Ten years from now I don't want us to remember Twenty20 as a passing fad, something that we enjoyed but mismanaged, ultimately orchestrating its demise. Ten, fifteen, twenty years from now I want us all still to be saying what a great form of the game it is, and how great it is that it's still producing packed houses.

In spite of those who complain that Twenty20 is ruining players' technical approach to the game, I think this is nonsense and that it's very clearly improved all aspects of the game, whether it's Test cricket, four-day cricket, 50-over cricket, 40-over cricket or whatever, because it's another form of the game. People say that it's not cricket. It *is* cricket – it's just another form of cricket. And good players need to be able to adjust and play all forms of the game, and what you're seeing now is a more expansive array of shots played not just in Twenty20, but also finding their way into the longer versions of the game. You're also seeing bowlers bowling with more variety, in all forms of the game because they've had to learn it in Twenty20. They basically now need a bigger selection of deliveries, whether it be a slower ball, yorker or whatever. Diversity and pushing the boundaries of your technique are now the name of the game.

The captains have also had to think on their feet even more, because it's such a quick game that if you're not up to speed the game passes you by. The overall quality of the fielding and running between the wickets has also had to improve and we're now seeing all of that translated into the other versions of the game.

Again, the purists might hark back to a time when someone could bowl a length ball just outside off stump and a batsman might let it go or just play a forward defence, look up, and acknowledge the bowler for the quality of the delivery. These days a length ball just outside off stump can just as readily disappear behind square leg into the crowd for six and that's why you've got to move with the times, the whole time.

As great as I think Twenty20 is, and as much as I hope to see it develop and go from strength to strength, I am equally passionate that it isn't to the detriment of longer versions of the game, and especially Test cricket. Twenty20 is currently bringing a considerable amount of money into the game, which is great as long as it's filtered down from the top to grass roots and back up again, but the unfortunate reality in life is that money talks and if Twenty20 gets itself in a position where it commands the greatest revenue in the game, then there'll be no prizes for guessing the prevailing form of the game on future fixture lists.

I also don't want today's youngsters – eight-, ten-, twelve-year-olds now but cricketers of the future – growing up with the sole intention of playing Twenty20. The mark of a great player is someone who can play all forms of the game. Coaches obviously have a big part to play in ensuring this happens, at all levels. I'm all for being inventive, whether it's paddle or reverse sweeping, switch-hitting or whatever. Those shots have got to be taught and that's fine, but so too have the basics, such as footwork and how to get onto the front foot and how to defend off the back foot – all the techniques that provide a solid base, and will ultimately facilitate a more expansive array of shots. It is essential and that must never be forgotten.

I'm yet to find a player who spends a lot of time at the crease if he can't stop the ball. Therefore there are always going to be specialist Twenty20 players: that will definitely be the case whether I like it or not. I just hope that that approach – whereby a player concentrates solely on a particular form of the game – will only apply to a handful of players. I'm a firm believer that the ambitious and truly great players will be able to shake it up with the ball whatever the situation in whatever kind of match, or, alternatively, bat for eight hours and score big 100s, but can also score 100 off 60 balls in a Twenty20 game if needs be. It is of huge importance that the coaches and cricket authorities across the world recognize this and do everything in their power to address it. In my view it starts with the four-day game – the obvious breeding ground for Test cricket – and so it's essential that it is still seen by everyone as vitally important.

In 2008 the county champions received £100,000 in prize money. In 2009 it has increased to £500,000. This can only be a good thing, as it's the ECB's way of maintaining interest in the four-day game, which might otherwise begin to wane with players aware of the opportunities now available in Twenty20. Some might say that the need to do this and pander to the mercenary modern cricketer leaves a bit of a bad taste in the mouth, but what must be remembered is that these are professionals plying their trade and making their living, so it would be naïve to think that finances do not play a part. The ECB should be praised for seeing that and acting upon it quickly, and should now implement a similar policy for Test cricket. The prize money needs to be increased so that we're not seeing players retire from Test cricket in their late twenties to spend the next five years picking up big bucks in Twenty20 across the world.

The balance needs to be just right. I want to see two windows come in in the calendar year when there's no international cricket, one window that allows all the world's best players to go and play in the Indian Premier League, and another window, during our domestic season, where everyone can come and play in the P20, so that there's no conflict and we don't find ourselves in a situation where players have to choose between playing for their country or succumbing to the financial lure of one of the big Twenty20 Leagues. That just isn't right, for the good of the game. It devalues Test cricket. The absolute priority for any player should be representing their country: should that ever change wholesale, then it would be a sad day for sport. Make no mistake, I understand that, as a professional sportsman, cricketers generally have a short career window and want to follow the money. It is therefore up to the ICC to address the balance and ensure we don't start seeing early international retirements and defections in the game. This includes ensuring all cricketing countries across the world don't suddenly start saying that they fancy a piece of the pie and setting up a league and putting further strains on fixture lists and player commitments.

Longevity is the key here. I don't want the people who are running the game to try to flood as much money into the game as they can as a way of creating a fantastic legacy for themselves, only for it to have more damaging implications further down the line when their very fleeting tenure – as far as the sport is concerned – has come to an end. It is essential that 100 years from now, Test cricket is still flourishing and that – although I imagine I'll be long gone – if I got the chance to ask my great-great-grandchildren whether they would rather have a one-day or Test cap, they would still say 'Test cap, thank you,' every day of the week.

As the current powerhouse of world cricket, India also has a huge part to play. In a way, the biggest part of all, as everyone is looking to them and how they are going to handle the crazy money pouring into the IPL and how – in spite of considerably more interest from the Indian public for Twenty20 and the one-day game – they don't lose sight of the importance of Test cricket. I'm all for bringing as much money into the game for the players as possible, but the right proportion of it must re-enter the sport at grass-roots level, as an investment in the future.

My successes in the Army are owing in great measure to the manly sports of Great Britain, and one sport above all – cricket.

The Duke of Wellington

The four-day Test Match debate

The idea of the four-day Test Match has been discussed. Exactly why, I'm not quite sure. Test cricket for me is going along very nicely. Other than the brief and unsuccessful period of the 'timeless' Test (see *Haven't we got a boat to catch?* on page 10), the Test Match has lasted in the same guise for over 140 years, which would suggest it's here to stay. Why would you want to change it to four-day? The main change in Test cricket over recent years is the run rate. Go back to the 1950s or 1960s and it would be perfectly acceptable for your side to come in at the end of the first day's play of a Test Match with only 150 runs on the board. These days it's usually in the region of 300. This is due to a number of things, some of which are seemingly simple. Take running between the wickets for example. If you compare this with the past, you just don't see players jog a one or turn an easy two into a long single like you used to. I know it doesn't sound like much, but over an innings it makes a huge difference.

The biggest change, of course, is the prevailing effect of Twenty20, the one-day Powerplay and prior to that, the 30-yard circle for the first fifteen overs. These have had an effect on the psyche of the modern batsman and consequently his approach to batting, even in the Test arena. Basically, whether we like it or not, the rate of scoring is increasing. Take the Australian Test side, for example, which currently scores, on average, in the region of 90 runs per day – more than they did a decade ago. They are the most extreme example, but there is a quicker Test Match run-rate across the board. This obviously enables teams to put on bigger scores more quickly, and in turn gives them more time to bowl the opposing side out. Consequently, we are seeing far fewer draws than in the past, which is a good thing in my view. Lessen the game to four days and you will see fewer finishes.

"

Who made them boring?

Richie Benaud, looking deadpan and straight to camera, responds to Geoff Boycott's call for four-day Tests because five days are, according to Geoffrey, boring

"

Haven't we got a boat to catch?

All Test Matches in Australia before 1939 were designated 'timeless', except for two Tests at Melbourne in 1881/82, which ended in draws after four days' play, and all continued until there was a result. There were 96 in all, 56 from 1877 to 1914 and another 40 from 1918 to 1937. The longest, in Melbourne in 1929, took eight days.

The first 'timeless' Test in England was between England and Australia at The Oval in 1912, when they met in the Final of the Triangular Tournament, but only four days were required. This experiment was not repeated until 1926, but even then the more congested fixture list in England limited 'timeless' Tests to the final Test of every Ashes series at The Oval up to and including 1938. The longest (lasting six days) was in 1930, after a day was lost to rain.

The first 'timeless' Test outside England and Australia took place at Kingston, Jamaica in 1930, when England and West Indies were level 1-1 and it was decided to play the final Test of the series to a finish. After ten days, including a rest day and two days lost to rain, England had a boat to catch and the match was abandoned as a draw.

Nine years later, England were in South Africa and leading 1-0 after three of the first four Tests of the series, each restricted to four days' play, had ended in draws. As

South Africa could draw the series, it was agreed to play the final Test at Durban to a finish. This became the most famous 'timeless' Test when, after twelve days, including two rest days and the eighth day being lost to rain, England again had a boat to catch. Despite England reaching a record-breaking 654-5 in the fourth innings and needing only 42 runs to win, the match had to be abandoned. It remains the longest first-class game on record, thanks to 103 from Nourse in six hours and four minutes, 125 from PGV van der Bijl in seven hours and eighteen minutes, 100 from Paul Gibb in seven hours and 31 minutes, and 216 from Bill Edrich in the longest innings of the match, lasting seven hours 40 minutes.

When first-class cricket resumed after the Second World War there was no interest in 'timeless' Test Matches and five days eventually became the standard length. Sometimes a sixth day has been added, but usually only if an entire day has been washed out or if it was the final match of a tied series. Even so, after nearly 1,900 Tests since 1870, only 83 have ever gone beyond five days, and only nine have lasted seven days or more.

One-day cricket is an exhibition. Test cricket is an examination.

Henry Blofeld

Test Match Stats

Batting

Highest innings total:
952-6 dec (Sri Lanka v. India, Colombo, 1997)

Lowest innings total:
26 (New Zealand v. England, Auckland, 1955)

Most runs in a day:
588 (England went from 173-2 to 571 all out and India scored
190 without loss, Old Trafford, 27 July 1936)

Fewest runs in a full day's play:
95 (Australia 80 and Pakistan 15, Karachi, 11 October 1956)

Most wickets to fall in one day:
27 (England 17 and Australia 10, Lord's, 16 July 1888)

Most sixes in an innings:
17 (Australia (753-6 dec) v. Zimbabwe, Perth, 2003)

Most sixes in a match:
27 (Pakistan v. India, Faisalabad, 2006)

Bowling

Most runs conceded by a bowler in an innings:
298 from 87 overs and taking 1 wicket while England scored
903-7 declared (L.O. Fleetwood-Smith for Australia v. England
at The Oval, 1938 – at least he got Wally Hammond lbw!)

There have been 37 hat-tricks in Test Matches, 11 of them by England bowlers

13 bowlers have taken a wicket with the first ball of their Test Match career, 6 of them England players.

Wicket-keeping

Most dismissals in career:
475 (Mark Boucher of South Africa, 453 catches and 22 stumpings)

Highest innings total without conceding a bye:
Tatenda Taibu for Zimbabwe against Sri Lanka (713-3 dec) at Bulawayo, 2004

Most byes conceded in an innings:
37 (Les Ames for England v. Australia (The Oval, 1934)

Fielding

Most catches in career:
168 (Steve Waugh for Australia, 1985–2004)

Most catches by a substitute in an innings:
4 (Younis Khan for Pakistan v. Bangladesh, Multan, 2001)

All-rounders

Most Player of the Match awards:
20 (J. Kallis)

Captains

Most matches as captain:
93 (A. Border for Australia, 1984–1994)

Most matches as England captain:
54 (Mike Atherton)

Umpires

Most matches as umpire:
128 (Steve Bucknor, West Indies, 1989–2009)

Batting

Fastest century:
70 minutes (Jack Gregory for Australia v. South Africa, Johannesburg, 1921)

Fastest century from fewest balls received:
56 (Viv Richards for West Indies v. England, St John's, 1986)

Fastest half-century:
27 minutes (Mohammed Ashraful for Bangladesh v. India, Mirpur, 2007)

Fastest half-century from fewest balls received:
24 (Jacques Kallis for South Africa v. Zimbabwe, Cape Town, 2005)

Slowest century:
557 minutes or 9 hours 17 minutes (Mudassar Nazar for Pakistan v. England, Lahore, 1977)

Most sixes in career:
100 (Adam Gilchrist, Australia, in 137 innings – Andrew Flintoff has hit 81 in 123 innings)

Number 11 top scoring in an innings has happened seven times, the most recent being Steve Harmison with 42 for England (304 all out) v. South Africa, Cape Town, 2005

An opening batsman has been dismissed by the first ball on the opening day of a Test Match 26 times

7 players have been dismissed 'handled the ball', the most recent being Michael Vaughan after scoring 64 for England v. India (Bangalore, 2001)

Bowling

Most balls bowled in an innings by an individual bowler:
588 (98 overs) with 35 maidens and two wickets for 179 runs (by Sunny Ramadhin for West Indies v. England, Birmingham, 1957 – this was after bowling 186 balls (31 overs) in the first innings and taking seven wickets for 49 runs)

Most ten-wickets-in-a-match:
22 (Muttiah Muralitharan for Sri Lanka, 1992–2009)

Most deliveries bowled in career:
42,020 (Muttiah Muralitharan for Sri Lanka)

Worst Test career bowling average:
129.00 or 8 wickets for 1,032 runs (by Asoka De Silva for Sri Lanka, 1985/91)

Extras

Most extras in an innings:
76 (while Pakistan scored 537 v. India, Bangalore, 2007)

Most extras in a match:
173 (West Indies v. Pakistan, Bridgetown, 1977)

ᦒ

Punishment to suit the times

Despite cricket having become a leaner, meaner, harder-hitting and faster game over the years, over-rates – the very essence of what determines the pace of play – are getting slower and slower. If you go back to the 1950s, 1960s, 1970s, sides were bowling around twenty overs an hour. These days, albeit with the customary drinks break, sides are bowling around 13½–14. Not being able to get 90 overs in a day is ridiculous and it needs to be addressed. There is enough money in the game now for the top players (through central contracts, sponsorship and so forth), whereby it is not such an issue to be fined some of a match fee for orchestrating a slow over-rate in order to force a draw. Besides, these days, although the public will never be aware of it, there is every chance that a sponsor allied to the guilty captain will pay the fine anyway. Financial punishment is just not a suitable deterrent any more. I'd like to see it dropped completely and replaced with a policy where, for every over fewer than 90 that are bowled in a day, ten runs are added to the batting side's total: 30, 40, 50 runs can change the state of a game and, as a result, the fielding captain would make sure his bowlers got through the overs at the necessary rate.

Of course there would have to be allowances for any time lost to the weather or bad light, and a percentage worked out for days when a side's innings comes to an end during a day. Umpires and match referees would need to be strong to make sure that the batting side wasn't slowing the game down on purpose too. I'm also not saying that teams should forgo their drinks breaks either. They're essential, as science tells us that concentration and performance levels drop with even mild dehydration. But even with regular breaks there is still plenty of time to get through a decent number of overs in a day and there's no doubt in my mind that this rule change would provide adequate incentive to keep the game ticking over at the right pace.

Cricket is sport, but it is also in the entertainment business, and we should never forget the people who pay to come and watch. They should be able to buy their tickets – some of which are over £100 now – knowing they are going to see a certain amount of play that day. You don't want to con your audience, because they are the lifeblood of the sport and its future welfare.

"

If the French noblesse had been capable of playing cricket with their peasants, their chateaux would never have been burnt.

G.M. Trevelyan

"

150 Years Ago

– *The Beginning of International Cricket* –

The first England cricket tour overseas was to Canada and the U.S.A in the autumn of 1859. The tour was organised by W. Pickering, an original member of Surrey County Cricket Club, who had emigrated to Montreal. He obtained guarantees of £1,300 from sponsors and arranged a short series of five matches against teams of 22 players, plus three exhibition games, in Montreal, New York, Philadelphia, Rochester and Hamilton.

The England team was made up of twelve professionals, including John Wisden and John Lillywhite. Fred Lillywhite accompanied the team as a reporter and took his printing press and mobile 'scoring tent'. It took the team two weeks to sail from Liverpool to Quebec before beginning a triumphant tour lasting 35 days, winning every match while travelling 7,500 miles and attracting large and fashionable crowds. After all expenses had been met every player took home £90 in time for Christmas.

The success of the North American tour persuaded potential sponsors that a similar tour to Australia could prove financially profitable and two years later the first England tour of Australia began.

<hr />

Dropping the World Cup

Whether apocryphal or not, one of the most famous comments ever made on a cricket pitch came from the Australian captain Steve Waugh in an epic Super Six clash between Australia and South Africa at the World Cup in 1999.

South Africa looked to be well on their way to victory in the game when, to make matters worse for the Australians, Steve Waugh popped a sitter straight to Herschelle Gibbs at midwicket. In his excitement at the prospect of inflicting what would probably have been the killer blow to Australian prospects, Gibbs tried to celebrate the catch too early, and as he went to throw the ball in the air, it spilled from his hand onto the ground.

Legend has it that, as Waugh passed Gibbs, he asked the distraught South African: 'How does it feel to have dropped the World Cup?' Whether it's true or not, we do know that Waugh then went on to an unbeaten and match-winning 120 with just two balls to spare, and then captained his country to World Cup glory a few days later.

"

I have on occasion taken a quite reasonable dislike to the Australians.

Ted Dexter

"

If it ain't broke, don't fix it

Test cricket as the bastion of the game and the advent and success of Twenty20 has changed a lot of people's opinion of what should fall between the two. As of October 2008 the rules in the 50-over game were changed so that the batting team can choose when one of the Powerplays are taken. This would suggest that the ICC is still keen to move with the times and adapt to the pressures being applied elsewhere by the success of Twenty20.

Some people are suggesting that we knock the 50-over game on the head. I wholeheartedly disagree with that, but can see that there is still scope to tinker with it if needs be. What is essential, however, is that any future amendment of the Powerplay or other rules does not dramatically swing the 50-over game in favour of the big-hitting batsman. It is imperative that in the middle part of the game we still see the skill of batsmen dropping the ball for a quick single or knocking it into gaps for two.

Those calling for the introduction of more or longer Powerplays are missing the point. There's a skill in beating the infield, there's no doubt about that, but it's easier to do than when people are set back on the boundary ropes and you're still trying to keep the scoreboard ticking over. Take the record-breaking South Africa v. Australia 50-over game at Johannesburg in 2006, for example, when South

Africa successfully chased down 434. Don't get me wrong, the number of fours and sixes hit that day was amazing, but you would want it to remain as such – a phenomenal achievement – and not become the norm. Leave that to Twenty20.

As I've already said, Twenty20 is great and at the moment everyone loves it, but the problem it faces is the fundamental downside to short versions of the game: this being that the shorter the game, the less time there is available for the game to fluctuate one way or another in a team's favour.

Of course there are more final-over finishes, which are obviously exciting, but the problem is that – prior to those – you are only likely to see the balance of power in the match change a maximum of two or three times. Many would say that the endless stream of boundaries in Twenty20 make the *entire* match exciting and if that's what you've come to see, then fine, I can't argue with that, but my point is about the strategy and flow of a game. In the 50-over game there's more time for things to happen: you could be 50 for three after fifteen overs, then have a long partnership and get it right back up to 200 for 4 after 40 overs, before ending up with 275 after 50. The duration of the game then ensures a strategy for how the opposing side chases the total down.

I'm playing devil's advocate here as a way of pointing out that there is room for all forms of the game and that it is essential they are kept apart. The day that the Test game is adapted to cater for the Twenty20 crowd or vice versa, or anything in between, then we'll have lost the game's diversity and it'll be a huge mistake.

"

Chadwick, Adam, Mr. (MCC museum curator)
Williams, Glenys, Mrs. (MCC historian)
Urn, Ashes, Mr. (ceramic pot on wooden plinth)
Garland, Laura, Miss. (Mr. Urn's spokesman)

Passenger list for flight to Australia for Ashes tour
25 September 2006

"

The best things come in small packages

At the end of the last domestic County Championship season, Somerset captain Justin Langer wrote in his BBC column:

'For years, people interested in cricket have quizzed me about the Sheffield Shield competition in Australia and, in my opinion, we have been able to boast about having the best first-class structure in the world.

'The intense, cut-throat system in the Australian domestic game has had the effect of not only producing great cricket, but more significantly, great cricketers. This, of course, has been one of the catalysts behind the long and sustained success of the Australian Test and one-day teams.

'Over the last six months, however, I have experienced competition in Division One of the county championship, which was tough as any domestic cricket I have played in my career.

'For many years, everyone involved in cricket in England has been striving, or at least talking about, ways to improve standards around the county circuit.

'And with the season now having come to a close, I can say without hesitation that English cricket should be proud of the standards in Division One – and I can see absolutely no need to change anything about it.

'Whispers have been circulating about changes to the county game, but these ideas seem crazy to me. At last county cricket is at a level that any other domestic competition around the world would be envious of, so why change it again?

'For the first time since I initially played county cricket with Middlesex in the late 90s my view is that any young player who is able to dominate in Division One will be better equipped than ever before to step up into international cricket.

'By way of examples, take two young players from Somerset, James Hildreth and Craig Kieswetter. They both found Division One to be tough, hard core, cricket this summer but the experience will make them mentally and physically more durable players in the future.

'When they get to the point of playing consistently well at this level I would be confident that they will be ready to take on the pressure of Test cricket.

'There hasn't been a single game I have been involved in this summer that hasn't felt like a cup final and the pressure associated with this is sure to produce better cricket and therefore tougher cricketers.

'This, in turn, should have the positive, knock-on effect of producing a consistently strong England team.

'Obviously there are still arguments about too much cricket, flat pitches and too many drawn games, and while these are valid points, the overall county game is stronger than I have seen it since I first played for Middlesex in the 90s.

'The ECB should keep looking to further strengthen four-day cricket and with the increasing importance of Twenty20, a commonsense approach must be adopted to keep the game as healthy as the bank balances over the next few years.

'On the whole though, cricket in England is definitely heading in the right direction.'

Praise indeed, and coming from the truest of Aussies about our own domestic set-up, suggests that we're doing something right! I admire and respect what Justin said, but personally I still think there's scope for change. There is no question that the standard of first division county cricket in this country has improved but why can't the whole system of domestic cricket get better still?

I would start by reducing the number of sides involved from the current eighteen to a maximum of twelve, ideally ten. We've currently got in the region of 400 first-class cricketers in this country, only a small percentage of which will have the ability or correct mental approach to play for England. This inevitably means there is a higher percentage of 'ordinary' cricketers, shall we say, plying their trade out there. If you lessen the number of teams, then there is the same-sized pool of players going for fewer places in the top echelons of the domestic game. Therefore the percentage of quality players goes up and with it the overall standard of play. If, ultimately, you're going to make it to international level, then playing at a higher standard can only enhance your game.

And you have to make it hard work to get to the top. Whether it's the top for your county or the top for your country, when you get there, you've got to know that you've achieved it, and not just coast along, take a salary each month for playing cricket at the current second division level. You need to earn the right to earn a salary to play, not just be given that right.

Of course, this revision of the county game would be dependent on there being a strong system below it – the breeding ground for future talent and the opportunity for emerging players to go up a level when the time is right. It works in the form of the grade system in Australia so there's no reason why it can't work over here as well.

It's all hot air though, really, as it will never happen. The counties all vote for everything to do with the domestic game and so it's turkeys for Christmas. No one is going to vote themselves out of business: why would they?

And while the counties still vote you won't see too many radical changes happening. We saw it to an extent with the original proposal for the English Premier League, which was franchised to 9 sides. Counties went straight on the defence and said 'no'. So, unfortunately, a reduction in numbers is not something we're going to see very soon, which is a mistake and a shame in my view. I'm all for making England the best side in the world – we just need to produce the correct breeding ground to do so.

In an England cricket eleven, the flesh may be of the South, but the bone is of the North, and the backbone is Yorkshire.

Len Hutton

County Championship

1890–1976 – Official Champions:
Yorkshire – 30 titles (with 1 shared)
Surrey – 16 titles (with 1 shared)
Lancashire – 8 titles (with 1 shared)
Middlesex – 6 titles (with 1 shared)
Kent – 5 titles (with 1 shared)
Warwickshire – 3 titles
Worcestershire – 3 titles
Glamorgan – 2 titles
Nottinghamshire – 2 titles
Derbyshire – 1 title
Hampshire – 1 title
Leicestershire – 1 title

1977–83 – Schweppes County Championship:
Middlesex – 3 titles (with 1 shared)
Essex – 2 titles (with 1 shared)
Kent – 2 titles (with 1 shared)
Nottinghamshire – 1 title

1984–98 – Britannic Assurance County Championship:
Essex – 4 titles
Middlesex – 3 titles
Leicestershire – 2 titles
Warwickshire – 2 titles
Worcestershire – 2 titles
Glamorgan – 1 title
Nottinghamshire – 1 title

1999–2000 – PPPhealthcare County Championship:
Surrey – 2 titles

2001 – Cricinfo County Championship:
Yorkshire – 1 title

2002–05 – Frizzell County Championship:
Nottinghamshire, Surrey, Sussex and Warwickshire – 1 title
each

2006–08 – Liverpool Victoria 'LV' County Championship:
Sussex – 2 titles
Durham – 1 title

Total official County Championship titles:
31 – Yorkshire (1 shared)
19 – Surrey (1shared)
12 – Middlescx (2 shared)
8 – Lancashire (1shared)
7 – Kent (1 shared)
6 – Essex and Warwickshire
5 – Nottinghamshire and Worcestershire
3 – Glamorgan, Leicestershire and Sussex
2 – Hampshire
1 – Derbyshire and Durham

Gloucestershire, Northamptonshire and Somerset have never
won the County Championship.

Longest period since winning the County Championship outright:
75 years Lancashire
73 years Derbyshire
36 years Hampshire
31 years Kent
20 years Worcestershire

17 years Essex
16 years Middlesex
12 years Glamorgan
11 years Leicestershire
9 Years Surrey
8 years Yorkshire
5 years Warwickshire
4 years Nottinghamshire
2 years Sussex
1 year Durham

⁓

Two-tier County Championship

From 2000 the county championship was split into two divisions of nine, according to the counties' final placings in the 1999 season. Movement between the two divisions at the end of each season was to be on the basis of three relegated from Division One and three promoted from Division Two. This was lessened to two up and two down from 2006.

In the nine seasons since this new system was introduced, Sussex have won the county championship Division One three times, Surrey twice and Durham, Nottinghamshire, Warwickshire and Yorkshire once.

Every county has been relegated at least once and eight have been relegated twice: Essex, Glamorgan, Hampshire, Northamptonshire, Nottinghamshire, Surrey, Worcestershire and Yorkshire.

Nottinghamshire and Worcestershire have won promotion three times, Essex, Glamorgan, Hampshire, Middlesex, Northamptonshire and Warwickshire twice. Since relegation Leicestershire have never returned to Division One and Derbyshire, who were among the nine counties originally placed in Division Two in 2000, have remained in Division Two.

"

A loving wife is better than making 50 at cricket, or even 99 – beyond that I will not go.

J.M. Barrie

"

Bradman

The 1936–37 Ashes series in Australia saw Donald Bradman captain the Australian side for the first time. People began seriously to question his appointment after England went

2-0 up in the series. Then Bradman chose to silence his critics. He scored 270, 212 and 169 in the next three Tests, with Australia winning all three.

It remains the only time in Ashes history that a team has won a five-match series having been two down.

In 1948, at 39 years old he led the Australian team on their first tour of England after the Second World War. His team became part of cricketing legend as 'The Invincibles', playing 36 matches including five Tests but remaining unbeaten on the tour. They won 27 matches, drawing only nine, including the 4-0 Ashes series victory.

At that time, no team had ever made more than 400 runs in the fourth innings of a Test Match to win. At Headingley, The Invincibles did just that.

The final day of the Test started with England on 362 for eight. England captain Norman Yardley decided that his side should bat for ten minutes before declaring to add a few more runs and also give himself the choice of roller between innings. He chose the heavy roller so as to break up the pitch and help his brilliant off-spinner Jim Laker. And so the scene was set: Australia required 404 runs to win in just 344 minutes.

Initially they fell behind, scoring just 32 in 45 minutes, before Lindsay Hassett was caught and bowled by Denis Compton, bringing Bradman to the crease. At lunch Australia were 121 for 1. Then came the onslaught. Arthur Morris and Bradman set about the English bowlers, hammering 301 runs in 217 minutes for the second wicket. Morris lost his wicket for 182 but Bradman, unbeaten on

173, guided them to their world-record target with ten minutes to spare. It was perhaps the most awesome display of batting Leeds will ever see.

The 1948 series is also known for one of the most poignant moments in Ashes history – in the fifth and final Test at The Oval, Bradman came to the crease for his last-ever Test innings, needing only four runs to retire with a career batting average of over 100. The English captain Norman Yardley called for three cheers for Bradman, and then shook him by the hand. Noticeably moved by the reception, Bradman took some time to compose himself before settling over his bat to face leg-spinner Eric Hollies.

Bradman played the first ball defensively, later saying that he hardly saw it, so stirred were his emotions. Hollies then bowled a googly at Bradman on a perfect length. Bradman went forward and got an inside edge onto his stumps. Unthinkably, Bradman was out, and his duck left him with a career average of 99.94.

It is, however, probably the only duck in cricketing history upon which the batsman has received a standing ovation from the entire ground on his return to the pavilion. They said goodbye to the greatest batsman that has ever lived.

Less is more?

The cricket bat has evolved and improved considerably over the years. The modern professional sportsman has also had to get stronger. Therefore the ball is being hit further. So why are boundaries getting shorter?

It is the same principle in golf, albeit much of the extra distance coming from a dramatic evolution of the ball, something that has not affected cricket for quite some time. Anyway, people now drive the ball much further than they used to, so in many cases, golf clubs have responded by moving the tees back. Why not do the same with boundaries in cricket, rather than what we're seeing in a lot of cases, where it is shortened in the belief that the paying public want to see a glut of boundaries?

I'd push them back and have a certain minimum length to the boundary rope strictly enforced. There are currently only ambiguous suggestions from the ICC on boundary lengths, and pretty much nothing in place to deter a groundsman from citing a first-class match on the edge of a huge square, should he wish to do so. With the understandably huge squares required today in order to cater for an increasingly busy fixture list, that often leaves a ridiculously short boundary.

If you hit the ball long then great, you deserve six. But if you don't get hold of it properly, then it shouldn't be a possibility to get a six. If you miss-hit it, the fielding side should have the opportunity to catch you, otherwise you're just being rewarded for a poor shot, rather than penalised for it. So I'd like to see boundaries pushed back to encourage a more diverse set of skills for batsmen. If you can't clear an 80- or 90-yard boundary then you can still put it up in the air but you might have to chip the ball deliberately into a gap beyond the infield, for example. It would force a lot of batsmen to think more and in turn, in spite of what a lot of people think, would actually produce more of a spectacle for the public, rather than in a lot of instances, a steady stream of relatively trouble-free sixes.

⧼⧽

Where watching cricket could damage your health

– *The Grounds with the Most Sixes* –

Limited overs

Top of the list of grounds with the highest ratio of sixes per 300 balls (50 overs) in ODIs since 1996:
AML Stadium, Christchurch, New Zealand with 204 sixes in 22 matches, ratio 5.10

In the top 10:
South Africa – 5 grounds
New Zealand – 3 grounds
Kenya – 2 grounds

The ground with the most sixes in ODIs since 1996:
Gymkhana Club Ground, Nairobi, Kenya with 356 sixes in
57 matches

The ground with the most sixes in all-time ODIs:
Sharjah, United Arab Emirates with 905 sixes in 198 matches

*Top of the list of grounds with the lowest ratio of sixes per 300 balls
(50 overs) in ODIs since 1996:*
Rangiri Dambulla International Stadium, Sri Lanka with
61 sixes in 26 matches, ratio1.28

In the top 10:
Old Trafford, Trent Bridge, Melbourne, Brisbane and Sydney.
11th on the list is Lord's with 88 sixes in 26 matches

Test Matches

*Top of the list of grounds with the highest ratio of sixes per 300 balls in
Test Matches since 1996:*
Eden Park, Auckland, New Zealand with 100 sixes in
9 matches, ratio 1.58

The ground with most sixes in Test Matches since 1996:
Antigua Recreation Ground, St John's, Antigua with 122 sixes
in 13 matches

Top of the list of grounds with the lowest ratio of sixes per 300 balls in Test Matches since 1996:
Trent Bridge, Nottingham with 33 sixes in 12 matches, ratio 0.40

Lord's is third on the list with 68 sixes from 23 Test Matches

The all-time record for the most sixes in a Test Match:
27 – Pakistan v. India at Iqbal Stadium, Faisalabad, in 2006

"

One-day cricket is like fast food. No one wants to cook.

Viv Richards

"

Rebels, Mercenaries and Moguls

Cricket courted some serious controversy through the 1970s and 1980s. A lot of people didn't like Kerry Packer and what he did for the game. I think the exact opposite. Every professional cricketer across the world that has bowled a ball or swung a bat since Packer's creation of

World Series Cricket in 1977 has him to thank for the sums they have earned or now earn. Some people thought it was wrong of the players to walk out on their national side purely for money. But the reality is that, at that time, players were not being paid a sufficient amount to make a living from cricket, and so it was simply too big a lure.

They went and the cricket authorities had to act. In England they pulled in Cornhill Insurance as Test sponsors, while similar deals were struck in other cricketing nations across the world. The professional cricketer has never looked back. Suddenly, some reasonable money started flowing into the game. Not by today's standards but considerably more than was on offer to players before Packer's venture. I know he did it for business reasons, so he could show cricket on his own Channel Nine following his rejected bid to secure the exclusive broadcasting rights to Australian cricket, but whether his intentions were mercenary or motivated by his love of cricket, it doesn't matter, as there is no question that it has had a beneficial long-term effect on the game.

Throughout the 1980s the game had to deal with the rebel tours to South Africa. With the tours well-sponsored by the South African government, I'm 99 per cent certain that if you asked every single individual from the English, Sri Lankan, West Indian and Australian sides that went on those tours, they would say that they went there for the money. They were professional cricketers and although the finances were improving within the game by that stage, year on year, they certainly hadn't reached anything like the money kicking around today. Bearing in mind that the career of a professional cricketer is a relatively short one, here was an opportunity for players to set themselves up for later life – and they took it.

With regards to the politics, what it did or didn't do for South Africa is a completely different issue. Some might say that they were wrong for going, as it effectively endorsed the apartheid regime. Others felt that it was ensuring the game didn't die in one of the best cricketing nations in the world. Or, perhaps a little more tenuously, that it was bringing more joy to the South African people. But I think, if you asked them all to tell hand on heart why they went, there would be few qualms in admitting that money was the driving force.

They knew the consequences before they went. A lot of players took it on the chin and served their subsequent ban before returning to play international cricket again. Everyone has their reason for doing things. For me the biggest achievement is playing for your country – a privilege you should never turn down, but then other people have different views. You might not agree with them, but nevertheless, you should respect them.

Many of them were in the twilight of their international careers and perhaps thought, 'well, I might not play for England again, I may only play for another year, so I'm going to go and earn five years' salary in South African Rand in a couple of months'. It's the same issue that the game faces today with the IPL. Players opted for early retirement from the international game in the pursuit of money – something that shouldn't be allowed to happen again.

"

That Glenn McGrath … what a bastard.

Mick Jagger, 26 August 2005

"

Consider all options

I think it'd be fair to say that no one predicted that Twenty20 would be embraced across the world, quite the way it has. Less than a decade ago, it didn't exist. As far as the professional game is concerned, it has come out of the blue. So what's to say that another form of the game might not enter the fray over the next decade? Why not Ten10, where everyone except for the wicket-keeper bowls one ten-ball over each? This would create the need for what I call 'the total cricketer' – the necessity to be able to bat, bowl and field all at the highest level in order to make it into a side.

Or perhaps in the future, with the aim of breaking into the US, you adopt the opposite approach and – emulating baseball – have eleven specialist batsmen, ten specialist bowlers and ten specialist fielders in a 30-strong team. A bowler comes on for his over and once he's completed that he leaves the field as the next specialist bowler comes out to the middle. All the while you have your ten specialist fielders on, who remain on for the duration of the innings. They don't bat or bowl, they're just ten amazing fielders, ten Jonty Rhodeses (if that's possible). Whereas now, there are the lower order who just about know which end of the bat to hold, and who come in and try to weed out a couple of runs. Instead you have eleven top-class batters, who don't field, don't bowl; they're entitled to, but on the whole they don't: scoring runs is what they're in the team to do.

Cricket is an open book and that's why it's great. We should never sit still and say 'there we are, we've done it, we've got everything absolutely spot on'. The possibilities for the game are endless and so if someone comes up with a new and exciting prospect then let's trial it and see what happens. As you can probably tell I'm all for allowing the game to evolve …

The Top Three Test Batsmen and Bowlers from each Test-Playing Nation

England

Batsmen:
Graham Gooch – 8,900 runs (from 118 Tests at 42.58)
Alec Stewart – 8,463 runs (from 133 Tests at 39.54)
David Gower – 8,231 runs (from 117 Tests at 44.25)

Bowlers:
Ian Botham – 383 wickets (from 102 Tests at 28.40)
Bob Willis – 325 wickets (from 90 Tests at 25.20)
Fred Trueman – 307 wickets (from 67 Tests at 21.57)

Australia

Batsmen:
Allan Border – 11,174 runs (from 156 Tests at 50.56)
Ricky Ponting – 10,960 runs (from 131 Tests at 56.20)
Steve Waugh – 10,927 runs (from 168 Tests at 51.06)

Bowlers:
Shane Warne – 707 wickets (from 145 Tests at 25.41)
Glenn McGrath – 563 wickets (from 124 Tests at 21.64)
Dennis Lillee – 355 wickets (from 70 Tests at 23.92)

South Africa

Batsmen:
Jacques Kallis – 10,277 runs (from 131 Tests at 54.66)
Gary Kirsten – 7,289 runs (from 101 Tests at 45.27)
Graeme Smith – 6,342 runs (from 77 Tests at 50.33)

Bowlers:
Shaun Pollock – 421 wickets (from 108 Tests at 23.11)
Makhaya Ntini – 388 wickets (from 99 Tests at 23.87)
Allan Donald – 330 wickets (from 72 Tests at 22.25)

West Indies

Batsmen:
Brian Lara – 11,912 runs (from 130 Tests at 53.17)
Viv Richards – 8,540 runs (from 121 Tests at 50.23)
Shivnarine Chanderpaul – 8,506 runs (from 120 Tests at 49.45)

Bowlers:
Courtney Walsh – 519 wickets (from 132 Tests at 24.44)
Curtly Ambrose – 405 wickets (from 98 Tests at 20.99)
Malcolm Marshall – 376 wickets (from 81 Tests at 20.94)

New Zealand

Batsmen:
Stephen Fleming – 6,875 runs (from 108 Tests at 39.73)
Martin Crowe – 5,444 runs (from 77 Tests at 45.36)
John Wright – 5,334 runs (from 82 Tests at 37.82)

Bowlers:
Richard Hadlee – 431 wickets (from 86 Tests at 22.29)
Daniel Vettori – 293 wickets (from 92 Tests at 33.55)
Chris Cairns – 218 wickets (from 62 Tests at 29.40)

India

Batsmen:
Sachin Tendulkar – 12,773 runs (from 159 Tests at 54.58)
Rahul Dravid – 10,749 runs (from 133 Tests at 52.95)
Sunil Gavaskar – 10,122 runs (from 125 Tests at 51.12)

Bowlers:
Anil Kumble – 619 wickets (from 132 Tests at 29.65)
Kapil Dev – 434 wickets (from 131 Tests at 29.64)
Harbhajan Singh – 330 wickets (from 77 Tests at 30.42)

Pakistan

Batsmen:
Javed Miandad – 8,832 runs (from 124 Tests at 52.57)
Inzamam-ul-Haq – 8,829 runs (from 119 Tests at 50.16)
Mohammad Yousuf – 6,770 runs (from 79 Tests at 55.49)

Bowlers:
Wasim Akram – 414 wickets (from 104 Tests at 23.62)
Waqar Younis – 373 wickets (from 87 Tests at 23.56)
Imran Khan – 362 wickets (from 88 Tests at 22.81)

Sri Lanka

Batsmen:

Mahela Jayawardene – 8,251 runs (from 102 Tests at 53.23)
Sanath Jayasuriya – 6,973 runs (from 110 Tests at 40.07)
Kumar Sangakkara – 6,764 runs (from 80 Tests at 54.99)

Bowlers:

Muttiah Muralitharan – 765 wickets (from 126 Tests at 22.12)
Chaminda Vaas – 354 wickets (from 110 Tests at 29.40)
Sanath Jayasuriya – 98 wickets (from 110 Tests at 32.40)

Zimbabwe

Batsmen:

Andy Flower – 4,794 runs (from 63 Tests at 51.54)
Grant Flower – 3,457 runs (from 67 Tests at 29.54)
Alistair Campbell – 2,858 runs (from 60 Tests at 27.21)

Bowlers:

Heath Streak – 216 wickets (from 65 Tests at 28.14)
Paul Strang – 70 wickets (from 24 Tests at 36.02)
Ray Price – 69 wickets (from 18 Tests at 35.86)

Bangladesh

Batsmen:

Mabibul Bashar – 3,013 runs (from 49 Tests at 31.38)
Mohammad Ashraful – 2,125 runs (from 48 Tests at 23.87)
Javed Omar – 1,720 runs (from 40 Tests at 22.05)

Bowlers:

Mohammad Rafique – 100 wickets (from 33 Tests at 40.76)
Mashrafe Mortaza – 78 wickets (from 35 Tests at 41.19)
Shahadat Hossain – 50 wickets (from 21 Tests at 43.76)

"

Batting for Viv Richards is a matter of strokes, more strokes, and even more strokes.

John Arlott

"

There's more life on Mars

The England side has recently returned from a Test series in the Caribbean which, at times, has tested the patience of those both playing and watching because of the batsman-friendly pitches that yielded an amazing seventeen centuries in all. On that occasion, as the West Indies were defending a 1-0 lead throughout the series (following England's bizarre capitulation at Jamaica, when they were bowled out for 51), some might say that the pitches were prepared purely for that purpose: to watch both sides rack-up scores well in excess of 500 over the first three or four days and effectively kill the game off. Cynical as that might sound, it doesn't really address the wider problem of bland pitches that are becoming more commonplace in the Test game.

Take Lord's, for example, the hallowed turf and home of cricket. I love the place but there is no avoiding the fact that it has recently played host to five consecutive Test Match draws. Coincidence? Or simply a pitch too benign to produce a finish? Unfortunately it appears the latter.

Since the late 1980s all natural soil pitches have gradually been replaced by those made from Surrey and Ongar loams. The problem being they are all gradually becoming one and the same thing. Commercial pressures to produce pitches that last five days are also playing their part – something detrimental to the game and, ultimately, to profitability, as fans gradually lose hope of seeing a finish and stop coming as a result.

Each pitch should have its own character. For example, say you go to Old Trafford, you know that it's going to reverse swing and turn; but then, if you go to Headingley, you know that it's going to seam about. If you go to India, many of the pitches are going to turn; if you go to Australia there'll be bounce … so wherever a Test Match is played, it will be different, and a diverse range of skills are required to cope with pitches around the world.

A decent Test pitch needs to offer a little bit from the outset so the new ball has got a chance of knocking over the openers. There should be consistent pace and bounce but there should be enough green on it for some movement off the seam. As the game goes on you want the pitch to dry out, but not too quickly so that it cracks up on days two and three. It should be good to bat on, on days one, two and three, before the surface begins to deteriorate on days four and five, and offer some turn so that the spinners can come on and create a new, exciting phase of the game. Old Trafford is good for this – although on occasions creating a little too much turn, it often delivers Test matches that produce a result after lunch on day five: that to me is the perfect Test Match.

Of course, it's impossible for a groundsman to engineer in what session a Test Match will reach its conclusion, but he can certainly influence it. It's a serious skill and one that I want to see groundsmen and their staff allowed to exercise properly, and not with pressure applied by the authorities to be cautious and produce a batsman-friendly track that will definitely see a full five days' play.

Another benefit is that we get to see the skill of the selectors having to pick a side based on the pitch. They will have had to read the pitch properly and then pick a team accordingly, hoping their selection can cope with any issues the pitch might produce, and therefore have the team to go and win. They certainly don't always get it right. I remember when we played at Eden Gardens in the First Test in 1993 and the England selectors picked four seamers and one spinner, whereas India went with two seamers and three spinners, and beat us by eight wickets. And then, in 1997, when we played Australia at Headingley and the selectors left out Andy Caddick for Mike Smith. It's traditionally an uneven surface at Leeds so you want a tall bowler to exploit the bounce and the selectors chose to leave out a six-foot six-inch bowler and picked a five-foot ten-inch bowler instead. We lost by an innings and 61 runs and so, with hindsight, you could say that both Tests saw radical selector errors. Anyway, it's just another interesting facet of the game, and one that generic and benign pitches shouldn't be allowed to negate in the future.

"

You are a damned lot of sneaks.

W.G. Grace to William Midwinter, England v. Australia,
The Oval 1877

"

Ball of the Century

You might think it somewhat difficult to pick out the single best delivery in a hundred years of cricket. Nevertheless, it's almost unanimously agreed that the 'Ball of the Century' came at Old Trafford in the first Ashes Test of 1993 – and more importantly, came from a hand delivering its first-ever ball in Ashes cricket.

After a slow and short run-up, a young and unknown Australian leg-spinner named Shane Warne arrived at the crease to deliver what appeared to be a normal leg-break to the facing right-handed Mike Gatting. It turned out to be anything but.

At first it flew straight, but about halfway down the pitch the inordinate spin on the ball caused it to drift to the right. As the ball arrived at Gatting, it dipped suddenly before pitching well outside his leg stump. Having successfully followed the ball's deviation down the leg side, Gatting knew he couldn't be out lbw, and so pushed his bat and pad forward into a conventional position to defend a leg-break of this kind. If it didn't hit his pad, then his straight bat would be in place to act as a second line of defence. Instead, the ball bit on the turf and spun back so much that it missed absolutely everything except Gatting's off-stump.

No one could quite believe what they had just seen, least of all Gatting, who – according to his captain Graham Gooch, who was batting at the other end – 'looked as though someone had just nicked his lunch'. As the Aussies celebrated around him, Gatting just stood there before finally setting off on his long walk back to the pavilion, most of which he spent shaking his head in sheer disbelief at it all. You can hardly blame him though: he'd just faced the best delivery in 93 years.

A list you want your name on

The year 2000 saw the introduction of central contracts – in my view, an absolutely brilliant addition to the structure of the game. It immediately ensured that the very best players in the country are all looked after and utilised in the correct way. Everything is monitored on a sensible level: the amount of cricket they play, their fitness, where and when they play ... it all has to be a good thing. As long as it isn't taken to the other extreme and they are wrapped up in cotton wool.

Take Steve Harmison, for example. He needs to bowl regularly to stay in rhythm, in order to deliver at his very best. It was no coincidence that he wasn't playing for England at the start of the summer in 2008; but, after putting in the necessary overs for Durham, he came back in the Oval Test Match against the South Africans in August to bowl at the level we know he can. On form he's probably still the best bowler in the world.

So all-in-all, central contracts have been great. You've just got to make sure that the coach, or whoever is in charge, works out what is best for each individual player. Should he go and play because he's on form – and keep playing – or is he the type of person that, if you give him a rest or a week off, will come back even better? These are questions the coach needs to consider and it's a skill being able to work out the correct answers for each individual player.

I think that the authorities also need to look at the financial side of things as well. If you secure a central contract you get a guaranteed salary a little higher than a top-class county cricketer. That's fine, as I'm a firm believer that you should reward the elite. The area I think that needs addressing is appearance money. It is currently set at around £5,500 for a Test Match appearance in England and £7,700 while on tour, when I think it should be increased to no less than £10,000. By doing that, you reward players for getting a central contract, but you further reward those top eleven players in the country. That way, there's a real desire – not just to earn a central contract – but to get one, and then ensure that you play as well. Again, it's about rewarding form and success, rather than mediocrity.

This theory would be enhanced further if the number of contracts handed out were to increase. I know that Tim Ambrose, Ravi Bopara, Samit Patel, Matt Prior, Owais Shah, Graeme Swann and Luke Wright have all received increment contracts, whereby they receive an additional one-off payment from the ECB on top of the salary they receive from their county, but it isn't the same. The twelve centrally contracted players are paid entirely by the ECB and so they have the necessary control over the players in order to apply a sensible monitoring process. The increment contracts are, in principle, the same as the previously awarded summer contracts and can now be won through a points system whereby five points are awarded for a Test appearance and two for a Twenty20 or ODI appearance with an England increment contract being awarded automatically once a player reaches twenty points during the twelve-month contract period.

Although I like the notion of a graded system that helps to encourage players further still to make that next step up, I do wonder whether this isn't complicating the issue a little unnecessarily and that the ECB wouldn't do better simply to award more central contracts instead, and therefore be able to exercise the level of control they would like over a larger pool of players.

The following twelve players have central contracts for the period from 1 October 2008 to 30 September 2009:

James Anderson (Lancashire)
Ian Bell (Warwickshire)
Stuart Broad (Nottinghamshire)
Paul Collingwood (Durham)
Alastair Cook (Essex)
Andrew Flintoff (Lancashire)
Stephen Harmison (Durham)
Monty Panesar (Northamptonshire)
Kevin Pietersen (Hampshire)
Ryan Sidebottom (Nottinghamshire)
Andrew Strauss (Middlesex)
Michael Vaughan (Yorkshire)

As with all international teams and squads that have been selected since sporting time began, the list of central contracts creates an amazing amount of debate. It is a twenty-first-century addition to the things that many a pub or armchair selector will no doubt disagree with or at least have something to say about.

This year it seems that the standard gripe was the inclusion of Michael Vaughan. Personally, I don't have a problem with him having a central contract as, when they were given out, he had only just stepped down from the captaincy following the loss against South Africa at Edgbaston, and made himself unavailable for one Test. Although he still hasn't made it back into the Test side, I think he still has a lot to offer international cricket. He just needs to string together a series of scores for Yorkshire and I have no doubt he will be considered again. They say form is temporary, but class is permanent, and there's no doubt that Vaughan has got class.

"

I'm a professional musician who plays the trumpet for a living, not some drunk trying to play the 'Last Post' on a didgeridoo.

Barmy Army trumpeter, Bill Cooper, after being evicted from the Gabba in Brisbane on 19 October 2006

"

Dodgy prawns

Partners, wives and families can be a distraction on tour if the amount of time they spend with players isn't controlled. Players are professionals, and like professionals in commerce and business, they and their families must realise they may have to spend time apart at certain periods during their careers. Those periods are not anything like as long as they used to be, as tours are much shorter these days. When I first started touring with England, we had to pay for our wives' or partners' travel costs and accommodation. During the 1995/96 tour of South Africa there was almost no restriction on time we could spend with our families and some players were definitely distracted. For the next tour Ray Illingworth banned all families from joining players in New Zealand and this went too far the other way. Management and players must find a balanced timetable that suits everyone.

I was always careful about food on tour. I never ate curries or any spice dishes. During the 44 days of the World Cup in Pakistan in 1996 I ate grilled chicken, mashed potato and broccoli every day! Some might consider that odd but I just didn't take the risk. Mind you, dodgy food on tour worked in my favour in Madras in 1992. When Gooch succumbed to a plate of bad prawns on the eve of the second Test, I got my first taste of international captaincy, with Richard Blakey replacing me behind the stumps. It turned out to be a baptism of fire. Sachin Tendulkar hit a century as India rattled up 560 for six – their highest ever total against England in India at that time. Although Graeme Hick, Neil Fairbrother and I got 64, 83 and 74 respectively, only one other batsman reached double figures and we were all out for 286. Enforcing the follow-on and spearheaded by a six-wicket second innings haul from Anil Kumble, they bowled us out for 252. We had lost by an innings and 22 runs. I'm glad to say I had more fruitful endeavours as England captain to come!

66 _____

A cricket tour in Australia would be the most delightful period in one's life, if one was deaf.

Harold Larwood

_____ 99

Circling vultures

When I was captain I usually attended Press conferences alone, sometimes with the tour manager. How times have changed, as these days England captains are given media relations training prior to their first exposure to the Press – and when they do speak to them, they are now flanked by a team of PR experts and cricket board hierarchy. I'm not saying that it's necessarily a bad thing, as there is always going to be the 'vulture' element of the Press corps, waiting for the slightest slip up to make something of. I didn't – or don't – resent them for it, they have their job to do and I'm prepared to listen to anyone's views on cricket, as long as they care about the game. That is essential though. If, ultimately, they don't have the best interests of the game at heart, then it's a very different matter.

I always read the newspapers and made a point of doing so in my playing days. The majority of players scour the newspapers, although a lot of them don't like to admit it. Obviously we don't like everything we read but I quickly learned not to tackle the Press head on unless absolutely necessary. You will never win taking on the Press. One or two of the current crop of players would do well to bear that in mind.

– *We cricketers will always spat with the Press* –

'I am not talking to anyone in the British media … they are all pricks.'

> Australian captain Allan Border's way of
> ingratiating himself with journalists during
> a Press conference while on Tour in 1993

'I didn't like to be friendly with rivals. I wanted them to feel the heat. And I didn't like reporters because you people think you know everything.'

Curtly Ambrose, 2 June 2006

'Gentlemen, don't believe all what you read in the media.'

Geoff Lawson to the Press, 2008

'I like king prawns with a bit of garlic. And I don't mind lobster. But "Vaughan the prawn" – what's all that about? Who writes these headlines?'

Michael Vaughan is perplexed by a *Sun* headline
– 'England captain shell-shocked as we faced battering'
– 22 July 2008

'If I had my time over again, I would never play cricket. Why? Because of people like you. The Press do nothing but criticise.'

Sir Gary Sobers 7 April 2004

'Test Match Special is all chocolate cakes and jolly japes, but I didn't enjoy being called a wheelie-bin, and nor did my family.'

Ashley Giles, 10 November 2003

'I don't know how they can figure out what's going on in my mind when sometimes I myself can't figure that out.'

Sachin Tendulkar on journalists, 17 October 2008

'I'm here to propose a toast to sports writers. It's up to you whether you stand up or not.'

Fred Trueman

❦

I'm not superstitious, but ...

Professional cricket is about doing everything in a professional way, to give yourself the best chance of dealing with whatever the game might throw at you. I made a point of always being as organised as possible and preparing in the same way. A habitual routine helped me deal with the pressure of the international game. I never slept well the night before the start of a Test Match or if I were due to bat the next morning.

I always arrived at the ground by 8.45am and had a net or throw downs before warm-ups and fielding practice and was back in the dressing room by 10.30am in preparation for the day's play. I wouldn't describe myself as a particularly superstitious person, just a creature of habit. Having said that, I would always step onto the field of play with my left foot first.

Oh, and I have to keep spinning the bat when I'm standing at the crease.

Oh yes … and I won't stand on any white lines …
Other than that, I'm perfectly normal!

But as you'll see, I'm not the only one …

Steve Waugh: carried a red handkerchief in his left-hand pocket, which had been given to him by his grandfather.

David Gower: never wore white socks.

Len Hutton: carried a five-shilling coin (crown) given to him by a friend of his grandfather.

Mike Atherton: would never give an interview or shave the next morning if he was not out overnight.

Denis Compton: carried a silver four-leaf clover.

Mark Ramprakash: always chewed the same piece of chewing gum throughout an innings. If not out overnight he stuck it on top of his bat for the next day.

Grant Flower and Mark Dekker: when going out to bat together always had the same conversation on their way to the middle – 'I hope you get hit on the head' followed by 'Same to you'.

Neil McKenzie: taped his bat to the ceiling of the dressing room when not batting and when going out to bat all the toilet seats had to be down. But in 2008 declared: 'I've got a wife and child now and don't have much time to worry about toilet seats and taping bats to the ceiling.'

David Shepherd: when the scoreboard showed a total of 111 (or 222, 333, 444, or 555) kept hopping until the score changed.

Slopes, stairs, history and Old Father Time

I bet if you asked every international, club or village cricketer across the world where they could play one last game, over 90 per cent would say Lord's. With my Surrey links, people would assume I would go for The Oval, but I wouldn't. I would be in that 90 per cent heading for St John's Wood. As much as I love the Oval, there is an element of playing there feeling a bit like just another day at the office, as it were, but Lord's has no comparison. From the moment you drive through the gates you can feel the history of the place. It has its own special atmosphere, the way you are looked after, everything just oozes quality and class. As soon as you get there you know that you are at a proper cricket ground. So for me it's not even a discussion point – it's Lord's and that's it. I've also had some decent success there, which obviously helps!

Although Lord's has changed considerably over the last couple of decades, with the modernising of several of the stands and obviously the new media centre, it doesn't matter how modern those new parts look, they could never detract from the history of the ground, the pavilion and all that surrounds it, all overseen by Old Father Time.

Looking up at the honours boards in the dressing room and seeing some of the great names up there – you want to join them, and it has inspired players for decades knowing that scoring a century or taking a five- or ten-wicket haul will see your name placed up there alongside your heroes forever. Walking down the stairs to the Long Room on your way out to bat you also have in the back of your mind that you're tracing their steps, walking through history. It's little things like that which add to the atmosphere and emotion of the place.

Also, trying to get through the Long Room packed full of MCC members on your way out to bat was always interesting. As you walk out, they clear the way, but as a lot of them are – how shall we put it – in their more senior years, some are a bit slower off the mark than others! Nevertheless, lots of them will wish you luck on the way out. If you do well you'll return to a room full of compliments, but if you get a duck you can hear a pin drop. Either way, the reception of the tightly packed MCC members is part and parcel of the place.

So is learning about and dealing with the slope. Although I've mentioned my concerns about all surfaces becoming a little too similar, the famous slope is a great little idiosyncrasy that sets Lord's apart. It needs mastering though, as it definitely affects the trajectory of the ball, as I found to my cost padding up to Glenn McGrath a few years ago. I let a ball go that I'd happily let go every time at pretty much any ground around the world. Instead, at Lord's, it removed my off stump. Nevertheless, I love the place. Always have. Always will.

Lord's – Home of Champions

One-day, limited-overs, single-innings competition Finals played at Lord's

Cricket World Cup winners:
1975 – West Indies
1979 – West Indies
1983 – India
1999 – Australia

Gillette Cup – 1963–80:
Lancashire – 4 wins
Sussex – 3 wins
Yorkshire – 2 wins
Kent – 2 wins
Middlesex – 2 wins
Warwickshire – 2 wins
Gloucestershire – 1 win
Northamptonshire – 1 win
Somerset – 1 win

Nat-West Trophy – 1981–2000:
Lancashire – 3 wins
Warwickshire – 3 wins
Essex – 2 wins
Gloucestershire – 2 wins
Middlesex – 2 wins
Derbyshire – 1 win
Hampshire – 1 win
Northamptonshire – 1 win
Nottinghamshire – 1 win
Somerset – 1 win
Surrey – 1 win
Sussex – 1 win
Worcestershire – 1 win

Cheltenham & Gloucester Trophy – 2001–06:
Gloucestershire – 2 wins
Hampshire, Somerset, Sussex and Yorkshire – 1 win each.

Friends Provident Trophy – 2007–08:
Durham – 1 win
Essex – 1 win

Total finals won at Lord's – 1963–2008:
7 – Lancashire
5 – Gloucestershire and Warwickshire
4 – Middlesex and Sussex
3 – Essex, Somerset and Yorkshire
2 – Hampshire, Kent, and Warwickshire
1 – Derbyshire, Durham, Northamptonshire, Nottinghamshire,
Surrey and Worcestershire

MCCA (Minor Counties Cricket Association) Knockout Cup:
Started 1983, became the MCCA Knockout Trophy in 1986
and first Final played at Lord's in 1990. Changed to the ECB
38 County Competition from 1999–2002 and back to MCCA
Knockout Cup from 2003–08.

Most wins:
Cheshire, Devon and Norfolk – 3 titles each

National Club Championship:
Various sponsors since 1969 and known as the 'Cockspur Cup'
since 1987

Most wins:
Scarborough – 5 titles
Old Hill – 4 titles

Village Cricket Cup:
Various sponsors since 1972 and known as the npower Village
Cup since 2005

Most wins:
St Fagan's (Glamorgan) and Troon (Cornwall) – 3 titles each

Ashes of what exactly?

'In affectionate remembrance of English cricket, which died at The Oval, 29 August 1882. Deeply lamented by a large circle of sorrowing friends and acquaintances, RIP. N.B. The body will be cremated and the Ashes taken to Australia.'

The first Test Match between the two countries had been played in 1877, but it was their ninth Test, and Australia's first and unexpected victory on English soil over a full-strength English side in 1882, that inspired a young British journalist, Reginald Shirley Brooks, to write this obituary in the *Sporting Times*.

A subsequent trip to Australia had already been organised prior to England's seven-run defeat, so three weeks later a team led by the Honourable Ivo Bligh set sail. Their objective was, as the English media put it, 'recovering the Ashes'. Although Australia hammered England in the First Test by nine wickets, England won the following two and so achieved their goal. This prompted a group of ladies from Melbourne to put some ashes in a small brown urn and present them to Bligh, saying: 'What better way than to actually present the English captain with the very object, albeit mythical, he had come to Australia to retrieve?'

For over a hundred years it was believed that the urn contained the ashes of a bail used in the third match, but in 1998 Bligh's 82-year-old daughter-in-law created considerable debate with the claim that they were the remains of her mother-in-law's veil instead. If that daughter-in-law and mother-in-law bit sounds confusing, it's because Bligh had gone on to marry one of the Melbourne women. In any case, other evidence also surfaced suggesting that it was the ashes of a ball. So, although the origin of the actual Ashes is the subject of some dispute, the passion with which they are contested has never been in question.

"

The traditional dress of the Australian cricketer is the baggy green cap and the chip on the shoulder.

Simon Barnes

"

The White West Indian

As well as Lord's, I also have a soft spot for Barbados. My two centuries there in the same Test in 1994 obviously contribute to that feeling, but it's definitely more than that. I had already played there in 1990, on my first tour of the Caribbean, and I loved it then as well. The pitch was usually good and suited my style of play, and the Bajans are great people. It was just impossible not to love their passion for the game. Also, when you do well out there, they take you to their heart. Because of the way I played, taking on the quicks, they all called me the white West Indian, which was a fine compliment.

Bridgetown always put on an excellent Test Match against England. Although the Kensington Oval holds only 14,000, the noise levels would be deafening, and the locals loved the travelling English fans, so there was always a cracking atmosphere.

Perhaps that's why it was so sad to see, on England's recent tour there at the beginning of 2009, the England supporters vastly outnumbering the West Indians, who seem to have deserted the game in droves. They say that the main contributing factor is the introduction of cable TV to the Caribbean. It means that their channels are now saturated with American sports and the younger generation is turning to basketball instead. Whatever the cause, I just hope that the West Indian drubbing of England at Jamaica in February 2009, when they bowled England out for 51 to win the First Test by an innings and 23 runs, will have a lasting effect.

Although much of the rest of the series was played out on batsman-friendly pitches, it saw an exciting conclusion and the West Indies held on for its first major series win in five years and the first time that they've won the Wisden Trophy in nine. I just hope that this long-awaited win is the necessary shot in the arm to set West Indian cricket back on track to the quality of its heyday.

Kensington Oval, Bridgetown, Barbados

First Test:
West Indies v. England, 1930

Tests played:
West Indies – 45 (won 21, lost 8, drawn 16)
England – 14 (won 3, lost 4, drawn 7)
Australia – 10 (won 3, lost 4, drawn 3)
India – 8 (won 0, lost 7 drawn 1)
Pakistan – 6 (won 0, lost 3, drawn 3)
New Zealand – 4 (won 1, lost 2, drawn 1)
South Africa – 3 (won 1, lost 1, drawn 1)

Highest innings:
West Indies – 749 for 9 declared v. England, 2009

Lowest innings:
India – 81 all out v. West Indies, 1997

Most runs:
Brian Lara – 1,339 (from 15 Tests at 53.56)

Most hundreds:
Clive Lloyd – 4 (from 9 Tests)
Desmond Haynes – 4 (from 13 Tests)

Most ducks:
Allan Donald – 3 (in 4 innings)
Chris Harris – 3 (in 4 innings)
Michael Holding – 3 (in 6 innings)
Wasim Akram – 3 (in 6 innings)
Pedro Collins – 3 (in 7 innings)
Mervyn Dillon – 3 (in 7 innings)
Ramnaresh Sarwan – 3 (in 18 innings)

Most wickets:
Courtney Walsh – 53 (from 12 Tests at 25.32)

Most catches:
Brian Lara – 25 (from 15 Tests)

Most Tests:
Brian Lara – 15

Most appearances as umpire:
Lloyd Barker – 11
Cortez Jordan – 11

You can always see at the SCG

The Sydney Cricket Ground is also great, again because of the atmosphere. Although it only has a capacity of 46,000 – unlike places such as Eden Gardens, which can hold 90,000, and the MCG, which can hold 100,000 – the atmosphere is better as the stands are closer to the boundary rope, and so the crowd is more on top of you. With some of the larger grounds, the fans can be set back too far away to generate a good audible atmosphere.

I've also had some entertaining times there performance-wise. Although it was bitter-sweet being adjudged lbw there just short of a century on my first Ashes tour in 1991, I very much enjoyed taking on Brett Lee at the same ground twelve years later to hit 71 from 86 balls in our first innings. Although we had already lost the Ashes, we went on to win the match by 225 runs and inflict Australia's first defeat on home soil for four years.

Sydney Cricket Ground, Sydney, New South Wales

First Test:
Australia v. England, 1882

Tests played:
Australia – 97 (won 53, lost 27, drawn 17)
England – 53 (won 21, lost 25, drawn 7)
West Indies – 14 (won 2, lost 10, drawn 2)
South Africa – 11 (won 1, lost 8, drawn 2)
India – 9 (won 1, lost 4, drawn 4)
Pakistan – 6 (won 2, lost 3, drawn 1)
New Zealand – 2 (won 0, lost 1, drawn 1)
Zimbabwe – 1 (won 0, lost 1, drawn 0)
ICC World Xl – 1 (won 0, lost 1, drawn 0)

Highest innings:
India – 705 for 7 declared v. Australia, 2004

Lowest innings:
Australia – 42 all out v. England, 1888

Most runs:
Ricky Ponting – 1,335 (from 14 Tests at 70.26)

Most hundreds:
Ricky Ponting – 5 (from 14 Tests)

Most ducks:
Glenn McGrath – 5 (in 15 innings)

Most wickets:
Shane Warne – 64 (from 14 Tests at 28.12)

Most catches:
Greg Chappell – 19 (from 12 Tests)

Most Tests:
Allan Border – 17
Steve Waugh – 17

Most appearances as umpire:
Bob Crockett – 11

"

My diet was sausages, then, in no particular order, sausages, chips, sausages, toast, sausages, beans, sausages, cheese, sausages, eggs, and the occasional sausage.

Marcus Trescothick explains his nickname 'Banger'

"

First class?

They've improved out of sight since I stopped playing but, when I was, I just didn't get how some grounds were granted first-class status. Certain out-grounds or club grounds, where facilities just aren't, or certainly weren't, good enough. I think if you're talking about first-class cricket it has to be a certain level on all counts and that's why I'm pleased that – as of 2010 – the universities are being stripped of their first-class cricket status. Although in sentiment it's a nice idea to give keen university cricketers a run out against professionals, the reality of these games is that the majority are very one-sided, with county professionals simply using them to massage their averages.

There are too many people walking around who have played one first class game for a university who were only picked because they didn't have exams that week, while the decent cricketer did. They shouldn't be first-class cricketers; you should have to work to get to that title in my opinion. And the same applies for a first-class cricket ground. You can stage a first-class cricket match, but only if the facilities are right. This includes the surface that you're playing on, the practice and dressing room facilities and everything that comes with those. Basically, the whole set-up should be at a level to cater for a professional sport and that certainly wasn't always the case in my time. There were one or two very ropey set-ups around. Maybe I'm just ranting because I never got a run at these places!

– *Wet, cold and miserable* –

County Ground, Derby

Established:
1853

Highest innings:
Nottinghamshire – 661 v. Derbyshire, 1901

Lowest innings:
Derbyshire – 26 all out v. Yorkshire, 1880

Highest score:
Billy Gunn – 273 for Nottinghamshire v. Derbyshire, 1901

10 wickets in an innings:
Richard Johnson – 10-45 for Middlesex v. Derbyshire, 1994

County Ground, Northampton

Established:
1885

Highest innings:
Northamptonshire – 781 for 7 declared v. Nottinghamshire, 1995

Lowest innings:
Northamptonshire – 15 all out v. Yorkshire, 1908

Highest score:
Michael Hussey – 329* for Northamptonshire v. Essex, 2001

~~~~

Where cricketing gods have plied their trade

– Test Match Grounds in England and Wales –

Lord's, London

First Test:
England v. Australia, 1884

Tests played:
England – 115 (won 42, lost 27, drawn 46)
Australia – 34 (won 15, lost 5, drawn 14)
West Indies – 18 (won 4, lost 7, drawn 7)
India – 15 (won 1, lost 10, drawn 4)
New Zealand – 15 (won 1, lost 6, drawn 8)
South Africa – 15 (won 4, lost 7, drawn 4)
Pakistan – 12 (won 3, lost 3, drawn 6)
Sri Lanka – 5 (won 0, lost 2, drawn 3)

Zimbabwe – 2 (won 0, lost 2, drawn 0)
Bangladesh – 1 (won 0, lost 1, drawn 0)

Highest innings:
Australia – 729 (for 6 declared) v. England, 1930

Lowest innings:
India – 42 all out v. England, 1974

Most runs:
Graham Gooch – 2,015 (from 21 Tests at 53.02)

Most hundreds:
Michael Vaughan – 6 (from 12 Tests)
Graham Gooch – 6 (from 21 Tests)

Most ducks:
Mark Ramprakash – 5 (in 13 innings)

Most wickets:
Ian Botham – 69 (from 15 Tests at 24.53)

Most catches:
Wally Hammond – 20 (from 12 Tests)
Colin Cowdrey – 20 (from 13 Tests)

Most Tests:
Graham Gooch – 21

Most appearances as umpire:
Dickie Bird – 15

Old Trafford, Manchester

First Test:
England v. Australia, 1884

Tests played:
England – 72 (won 24, lost 14, drawn 34)
Australia – 29 (won 8, lost 7, drawn 14)
West Indies – 15 (won 5, lost 6, drawn 4)
South Africa – 9 (won 1, lost 4, drawn 4)
India – 8 (won 0, lost 3, drawn 5)
New Zealand – 7 (won 0, lost 3, drawn 4)
Pakistan – 5 (won 1, lost 1, drawn 3)
Sri Lanka – 1 (won 0, lost 1, drawn 0)

Highest innings:
Australia – 656 (for 8 declared) v. England, 1964

Lowest innings:
India – 58 all out v. England, 1952

Most runs:
Denis Compton – 818 (from 8 Tests at 81.80)

Most hundreds:
Gordon Greenidge – 3 (from 4 Tests)
Denis Compton – 3 (from 8 Tests)
Alec Stewart – 3 (from 9 Tests)

Most ducks:
Graham Thorpe – 4 (in 13 innings)

Most wickets:
Alec Bedser – 51 (from 7 Tests at 13.45)

Most catches:
Jack Ikin – 11 (from 3 Tests)
Wally Hammond – 11 (from 10 Tests)

Most Tests:
Godfrey Evans – 11

Most appearances as umpire:
Frank Chester – 11

Headingley, Leeds

First Test:
England v. Australia, 1899

Tests played:
England – 68 (won 30, lost 21, drawn 17)
Australia – 23 (won 8, lost 7, drawn 8)
South Africa – 12 (won 3, lost 6, drawn 3)
West Indies – 12 (won 6, lost 5, drawn 1)
Pakistan – 9 (won 1, lost 5, drawn 3)
India – 6 (won 2, lost 3, drawn 1)
New Zealand – 6 (won 1, lost 4, drawn 1)

Highest innings:
Australia – 653 (for 4 declared) v. England, 1993

Lowest innings:
West Indies – 61 all out v. England, 2000

Most runs:
Don Bradman – 963 (from 4 Tests at 192.60)

Most hundreds:
Don Bradman – 4 (from 4 Tests)
Geoff Boycott – 4 (from 10 Tests)

Most ducks:
Andrew Flintoff – 4 (in 9 innings)
Derek Underwood – 4 (in 13 innings)

Most wickets:
Fred Trueman – 44 (from 9 Tests at 18.06)

Most catches:
Colin Cowdrey – 16 (from 8 Tests)

Most Tests:
Graham Gooch – 12

Most appearances as umpire:
David Constant – 8

Edgbaston, Birmingham

First Test:
England v. Australia, 1902

Tests played:
England – 43 (won 22, lost 8, drawn 13)
Australia – 12 (won 3, lost 5, drawn 4)
West Indies – 8 (won 4, lost 2, drawn 2)
Pakistan – 6 (won 0, lost 3, drawn 3)
South Africa – 6 (won 1, lost 2, drawn 3)
India – 5 (won 0, lost 4, drawn 1)
New Zealand – 4 (won 0, lost 4, drawn 0)
Sri Lanka – 2 (won 0, lost 2, drawn 0)

Highest innings:
England – 633 (for 5 declared) v. India, 1979

Lowest innings:
England – 89 all out v. West Indies, 1995

Most runs:
David Gower – 767 (from 9 Tests at 59.00)

Most hundreds:
Mike Gatting – 3 (from 5 Tests)
Marcus Trescothick – 3 (from 6 Tests)
Colin Cowdrey – 3 (from 8 Tests)

Most ducks:
Jason Gillespie – 3 (in 5 innings)
R.C. Russell – 3 (in 7 innings)
M.J.K. Smith – 3 (in 7 innings)
Mark Ramprakash – 3 (in 8 innings)
Darren Gough – 3 (in 9 innings)
Graham Gooch – 3 (in 16 innings)

Most wickets:
Fred Trueman – 39 (from 7 Tests at 20.46)

Most catches:
Graham Thorpe – 12 (from 8 Tests)

Most Tests:
Alec Stewart – 11

Most appearances as umpire:
Charlie Elliott – 8

Trent Bridge, Nottingham

First Test:
England v. Australia, 1899

Tests played:
England – 54 (won 17, lost 16, drawn 21)
Australia – 21 (won 7, lost 4, drawn 10)
New Zealand – 9 (won 1, lost 6, drawn 2)
South Africa – 9 (won 2, lost 4, drawn 3)
West Indies – 8 (won 4, lost 0, drawn 4)
India – 4 (won 1, lost 1, drawn 2)
Pakistan – 3 (won 0, lost 2, drawn 1)
Sri Lanka – 1 (won 1, lost 0, drawn 0)
Zimbabwe – 1 (won 0, lost 0, drawn 1)

Highest innings:
England – 658 (for 8 declared) v. Australia, 1938

Lowest innings:
South Africa – 88 all out v. England, 1960

Most runs:
Mike Atherton – 1,083 (from 11 Tests at 60.16)

Most hundreds:
Denis Compton – 5 (from 7 Tests)
Mike Atherton – 5 (from 11 Tests)

Most ducks:
Rodney Marsh – 3 (in 6 innings)
Shane Warne – 3 (in 6 innings)
Bob Woolmer – 3 (in 6 innings)
Geoff Boycott – 3 (in 17 innings)

Most wickets:
Alec Bedser – 41 (from 6 Tests at 20.21)

Most catches:
Wally Hammond – 13 (from 4 Tests)

Most Tests:
Mike Atherton – 11

Most appearances as umpire:
Frank Chester – 7
David Constant – 7

Kennington Oval, London

First Test:
England v. Australia, 1880

Tests played:
England – 91 (won 37, lost 18, drawn 36)
Australia – 34 (won 6, lost 15, drawn 13)
West Indies – 16 (won 6, lost 7, drawn 3)
South Africa – 13 (won 0, lost 6, drawn 7)
India – 10 (won 1, lost 2, drawn 7)
New Zealand – 9 (won 1, lost 4, drawn 4)
Pakistan – 8 (won 3, lost 3, drawn 2)
Sri Lanka – 1 (won 1, lost 0, drawn 0)

Highest innings:
England – 903 (for 7 declared) v. Australia, 1938

Lowest innings:
Australia – 44 all out v. England, 1896

Most runs:
Len Hutton – 1,521 (from 12 Tests at 89.47)

Most hundreds:
Herbert Sutcliffe – 5 (from 7 Tests)

Most ducks:
Alec Bedser – 5 (in 7 innings)

Most wickets:
Ian Botham – 52 (from 11 Tests at 26.51)

Most catches:
Ian Botham – 19 (from 11 Tests)

Most Test Matches:
Denis Compton – 13

Most appearances as umpire:
Frank Chester – 12

Riverside Ground, Chester-le-Street, Durham

First Test:
England v. Zimbabwe, 2003

Tests played:
England – 3 (won 3, lost 0, drawn 0)
West Indies – 1 (won 0, lost 1, drawn 0)
Zimbabwe – 1 (won 0, lost 1, drawn 0)
Bangladesh – 1 (won 0, lost 1, drawn 0)

Highest innings:
England – 447 (for 3 declared) v. Bangladesh, 2005

Lowest innings:
Zimbabwe – 94 all out v. England, 2003

Most runs:
Shivnarine Chanderpaul – 206 (from 1 Test at 206.00)

Most hundreds:
Shivnarine Chanderpaul – 1 (from 1 Test)
Paul Collingwood – 1 (from 1 Test)
Marcus Trescothick – 1 (from 1 Test)
Ian Bell – 1 (from 2 Tests)

Most ducks:
Mark Vermeulen – 2 (in 2 innings)

Most wickets:
Steve Harmison – 16 (from 3 Tests at 23.18)

Most catches:
Sean Ervine – 2 (from 1 Test)
Dwayne Bravo – 2 (from 1 Test)
Paul Collingwood – 2 (from 1 Test)
Ryan Sidebottom – 2 (from 1 Test)
Graham Thorpe – 2 (from 1 Test)
Andrew Strauss – 2 (from 2 Tests)
Marcus Trescothick – 2 (from 2 Tests)

Most Tests:
Steve Harmison – 3
Michael Vaughan – 3

Most appearances as umpire:
Aleem Dar – 1
Billy Bowden – 1
Darrell Hair – 1
Daryl Harper – 1
Tony Hill – 1
David Orchard – 1

Bramall Lane, Sheffield

First and only Test:
England v. Australia, 1902 (which Australia won by 143 runs)

Ground now converted into Sheffield United FC's dedicated stadium

Sophia Gardens, Cardiff

First scheduled Test:
England v. Australia, 8–12 July, 2009

⌘

They always seem to turn up at Kennington

I played against some great sides in my career – not least of all the brilliant West Indies side I made my Test debut against at Jamaica in 1990 – but there are two others that really stand out and both, funnily enough, at the Oval. The first of these was another West Indian side in 1991, this time with Curtly Ambrose in its armoury. It was only my thirteenth Test and we were trailing them 2-1 in the series when we went to the Oval for the final Test. In what was deemed by some to be a big selection gamble, my batting was preferred to Jack Russell's skills behind the stumps. I had done the job before at Adelaide and Perth the previous winter, although with less at stake. Anyway, I'd like to think that I didn't let anyone down, taking four catches in the match and contributing important innings of 31 and 38 not out, and we won by five wickets.

Despite our win – and the fact that we avoided a series defeat against the West Indies for the first time in eighteen years – make no mistake, they were one of the greatest sides there has ever been.

– *England v. West Indies* –

The Oval
8–12 August 1991
England won by 5 wickets to square the series 2-2

Philip Simmons
26 Test Matches: 1,002 runs; 1 century; highest score 110;
average 22.26; 26 catches; 4 wickets; average 64.25

Desmond Haynes
116 Test Matches: 7,487 runs; 18 centuries; highest score 184;
average 49.99; 65 catches; 1 wicket; average 8.00

Clayton Lambert (Test debut)
5 Test Matches: 284 runs; 1 century; highest score 104; average
31.55; 8 catches; 1 wicket; average 5.00

(Lambert was making his Test debut in place of the injured
Augustine Logie, who had played in the previous 4 Tests of
the series.

Augustine Logie
52 Test Matches: 2,470 runs; 2 centuries; highest score 130;
average 35.79; 57 catches)

Richard Richardson
86 Test Matches: 5,949 runs; 16 centuries; highest score 194;
average 44.39; 90 catches

Carl Hooper
102 Test Matches: 5,762 runs; 13 centuries; highest score 233;
average 36.46; 115 catches; 114 wickets; average 49.42

Viv Richards
121 Test Matches: 8,540 runs; 24 centuries; highest score 291;
average 50.23; 122 catches; 32 wickets; average 61.37

(This was Richards' farewell Test. His last innings c Morris
b Lawrence 60)

Jeffrey Dujon
81 Test Matches: 3,322 runs; 5 centuries; highest score 139;
average 31.94; 267catches/5 stumpings

Malcolm Marshall
81 Test Matches: 1,810 runs; highest score 92; average 18.85;
25 catches; 376 wickets; average 20.94

Curtly Ambrose
98 Test Matches: 1,439 runs; highest score 53; average 12.40;
18 catches; 405 wickets; average 20.99

Courtney Walsh
132 Test Matches: 936 runs; highest score 30*; average 7.54:
29 catches; 519 wickets; average 24.44

Patrick Patterson
28 Test Matches: 145 runs; highest score 21*; average 6.59; 5
catches; 93 wickets; average 30.90

(Ian Allen had replaced an injured Patterson in the Second
and Third Tests of the series. These would be the only two
Tests played by Ian Allen in his career – 2 Test Matches: 5 runs;
highest score 4*; 1 catch; 5 wickets; average 36.00)

I played against an equally – if not more – talented
Australian side at the Oval in 2001. Unfortunately *they*
handed out a cricketing lesson this time, winning by an

innings and 25 runs. We put on 432 in our first innings – not a bad score. The problem was they had already declared on 641 with only four wickets down and then bowled us out for 184, having made us follow on. On days one and two, Justin Langer, Mark and Steve Waugh all reached 100 in 177, 161 and 190 balls respectively. And on day three I became Shane Warne's 400th Test wicket. To rub salt in the wound, he got me out again in the second innings.

It's difficult to deal with, losing to any side in a Test Match – especially when you get thrashed. And worse still by the Aussies. But it was difficult not to admire a team comprised of some of the greatest players that have ever graced the game.

– *England v. Australia* –

The Oval
23–27 August 2001
Australia won by an innings and 25 runs
Australia won the series 4-1 and had already retained the Ashes after the first three Tests with only eleven days' play required.

Matthew Hayden
103 Test Matches: 8,625 runs; 30 centuries; highest score 380; average 50.73; 128 catches

Justin Langer
105 Test Matches: 7,696 runs; 23 centuries; highest score 250;
average 45.27; 73 catches

(Langer replaced Michael Slater in this Test. Slater had played
in all previous four Tests of the series. Michael Slater – 74 Test
Matches: 5,312 runs; 14 centuries; highest score 219; average
42.83; 33 catches; 1 wicket; average 10.00)

Ricky Ponting
131 Test Matches: 10,960 runs; 37 centuries; highest score 257;
average 56.20; 148 catches; 5 wickets; average 48.20

Mark Waugh
128 Test Matches: 8,029 runs; 20 centuries; highest score 153*;
average 41.81; 181 catches: 59 wickets; average 41.16

Steve Waugh
168 Test Matches: 10,927 runs; 32 centuries; highest score 200;
average 51.06; 112 catches; 92 wickets; average 37.44

Adam Gilchrist
96 Test Matches: 5,570 runs; 17 centuries; highest score 204*;
average47.60; 379 catches/37 stumpings

Damien Martyn
67 Test Matches: 4,406 runs; 13 centuries; highest score 165;
average 46.37; 36 catches; 2 wickets; average 84.00

Shane Warne
145 Test Matches; 3,154 runs; highest score 99; average 17.32;
125 catches; 708 wickets; average 25.41

Brett Lee
76 Test Matches: 1,451 runs; highest score 64; average 20.15;
23 catches; 310 wickets; average 30.81

Jason Gillespie
71 Test Matches: 1,218 runs; 1 century; highest score 201*;
average 18.73; 27 catches; 259 wickets; average 26.13

Glenn McGrath
124 Test Matches: 641 runs; highest score 61; average 7.36;
38 catches; 563 wickets; average 21.64

Some statistical comparisons between the two teams:

Runs scored:
Australia – 62,665
West Indies – 36,676

Centuries scored:
Australia – 173
West Indies – 78

Wickets taken:
Australia – 1998
West Indies – 1,545

Although the Australians clearly come out on top in all categories, stats don't always tell the whole story. Looking back I can say as a batsman I am still not sure who I would rather face, an Australian bowling line-up made up of McGrath, Lee, Gillespie, Warne and the Waugh brothers or the West Indian strike force of Ambrose, Marshall, Walsh, Patterson, Hooper and Richards. With the exception of Warne, of course, who got me out fourteen times during his career! Unfortunately, I can lay claim to being his most frequent victim, three of those wickets securing his landmarks of 150, 250 and 400 Test wickets!

As we all know, Warne was one of the best bowlers that the world has ever seen. But I think – had the Australian Cricket Board not deemed him such a liability as a consequence of his alleged off-field activities and constant portrayal in the media – then they would have made him captain. And there is no doubt in my mind that he would have been the best captain of his era. He definitely had the best cricketing brain. When he briefly got to captain Australia in the one-dayers in 1998 he was outstanding. Look what happened with the unfancied Rajasthan Royals that he coached and captained to win the inaugural IPL. There is no question that they punched above their weight in that tournament and came out as champions. Not only does he have a great cricketing brain, he is clearly an inspirational leader as well.

⌇⌇⌇

Feathery carnage

In 1999 Australia met India at The Oval in a Super Six match. It soon became apparent that, other than trying to progress to the semi-finals, both sides were doing their best to rid London of its pigeons as well.

An extraordinary ten minutes got under way when the ball was hit down to Aussie medium pacer Paul Reiffel at the third-man boundary. Reiffel picked up the ball and threw it back into the stumps – only for it to knock a passing bird from the sky, allowing the Indian batsmen to grab another run.

Then, while on 99, India's Ajay Jadeja cut a ball that looked set to evade all the Aussie fielders and bring up his century, except another pigeon had chosen to stand in its way. Although it brilliantly saved the single and denied Jadeja his century, the bird gave its life in the process.

Among all the feathery carnage, Jadeja eventually made it to a century, but that didn't stop the Australians winning by 77 runs.

◦◦◦

Partners in crime

Before I began to keep wicket full-time for England and was moved down the batting order, I opened the batting with Mike Atherton 50 times in Test cricket. Our partnership was one of the biggest strengths of English cricket during that period. We put on 1,930 runs together at an average of 38.60 and in those innings we shared six century partnerships, the highest of which was 171 against the West Indies at Bridgetown in 1993/94.

The stats might not be amazing but we definitely had a good understanding. Your opening partner is someone that you need to have a good relationship with. There's more to it than just running between the wickets; it's about knowing each other's game. Knowing how your partner reacts in certain situations so if things are going well, they can calm you down, but if things aren't going well they know how to build your confidence instead.

It was the same with Graham Thorpe, who I played a lot of cricket with at Surrey and for England. We had 31 Test Match partnerships, put on 1,024 together at 33.32. We had five half-century partnerships and two century partnerships, the highest of which was 150, in the same match as the opening partnership with Atherton at Bridgetown in 1993/94.

―――

The aim of English cricket is, in fact, mainly to beat Australia.

Jim Laker

The Ashes in stats

Ashes series:
63

Series won by England:
28

Series won by Australia:
31

Series drawn.
4

The quickest Ashes century was hit by Englishman Gilbert Jessop at The Oval in 1902. It took him just 75 minutes.

As something of a contrast, his later compatriot Geoff Miller took over two hours to make 7 on the 1978/79 trip to Australia.

The highest Ashes innings total is England's 903 for 7 declared at The Oval in 1938.

The lowest Ashes innings total is Australia's 36 all out at Edgbaston in 1902.

When England made Australia follow on at Trent Bridge in 2005, it was the first time they had suffered such ignominy in 191 Tests!

Australians have scored 276 centuries in Ashes Tests, 23 of them double centuries, while Englishmen have managed just 220 centuries, with only eleven of them being converted into double centuries.

Australian bowlers have taken ten wickets in a match 43 times, while English bowlers are just behind, having achieved the feat on 38 different occasions.

Fastest hundred (in terms of balls received where recorded):
56 balls, Adam Gilchrist (Australia), Perth, 2006/07

Fastest fifty:
27 minutes, Jack Brown (England), Melbourne, 1894/95

Fastest double hundred:
214 minutes, Don Bradman (Australia), Leeds, 1930

Fastest triple-hundred:
336 minutes, Don Bradman (Australia), Leeds, 1930

Most hundreds for England:
12 Jack Hobbs

Most hundreds for Australia:
19 Don Bradman

Highest individual innings:
364 Len Hutton (England), The Oval, 1938

Most runs in a day:
309 Don Bradman (Australia), Leeds, 1930

Most runs in a series:
974 (average 139.4) Don Bradman (Australia), 1930

Highest partnership:
451 (second wicket) Bill Ponsford and Don Bradman
(Australia), The Oval, 1934

Highest fourth-innings total (to win):
404-3 Australia, Leeds, 1948

Highest fourth-innings total (to lose):
417 (lost by 45 runs) England, Melbourne, 1976/77

Most runs in a day by one side:
475-2 Australia, The Oval, 1934.

Highest aggregate runs in a Test:
1753 (6 days), Adelaide, 1920/21

Lowest aggregate runs in a Test (all 40 wickets):
291, Lord's, 1888

Fewest runs in a full day's play:
106 (England from 92-2 to 198 all out), Brisbane, 1958/59

Largest victory:
An innings and 579 runs (England 903-7 dec. Australia 201
and 123), The Oval, 1938

Largest victory by runs:
675 (England 521 and 342-8 dec. Australia 122 and 66),
Brisbane, 1928/29

Most wickets to fall in a day:
27 (England from 18-3 to 53 and 62. Australia 60), Lord's, 1888

Most wickets in an innings:
10-53, Jim Laker (England), Old Trafford, 1956

Most wickets in a Test:
19-90, Jim Laker, Old Trafford, 1956

Most wickets in a series:
46 (average 9.60), Jim Laker, 1956

Hat-tricks for England:
4, Billy Bates (Melbourne, 1882/83), Johnny Briggs (Sydney, 1891/92), Jack Hearne (Leeds, 1899), and Darren Gough (Sydney, 1998/99)

Hat-tricks for Australia:
4, Fred Spofforth (Melbourne, 1878/79), Hugh Trumble (Melbourne, 1901/02 and 1903/04), and Shane Warne (Melbourne, 1994/95)

Bowler with most wickets:
195 (average 23.25) Shane Warne (Australia)

Most dismissals by a wicket-keeper in a series:
28 (all caught) Rod Marsh (Australia) 1982/83

Most dismissals by a wicket-keeper:
148 (141 caught 7 stumped) Rod Marsh (42 Tests, Australia)

Most catches in a Test:
7, Greg Chappell (Australia) Perth, 1974/75

Most catches in a series:
15, Jack Gregory (Australia) 1920/21

Banked moments

I was fortunate enough to represent my country at both one-day and Test level. I played in a lot of great matches (some stinkers as well!) but I can safely say that you never quite replicate the feeling you get on your Test debut. It's something that I constantly dreamed about as a youngster, worked tirelessly towards as a young professional and when you go out there for the first time playing for your country … well there is no better feeling. It just so happened that my debut Test turned out to be one of the most unlikely English wins of all time. England had just been thrashed by Australia in the Ashes, and with a number of leading players missing on a South African rebel tour, prospects didn't look too good as we arrived to face the West Indies at Sabina Park in the First Test. However, under Graham Gooch's captaincy, Devon Malcolm, Angus Fraser, David Capel and Gladstone Small all did their bit with the ball, Allan Lamb hit a gutsy century and we won by nine wickets.

Although my contribution was modest (batting at number three I only made thirteen in the first innings) the fact that it was my international Test debut – and we won – made it a match I'll never forget. Plus, I was at the crease when Wayne Larkins cracked the winning runs on the final morning, which made it even more memorable. Because I was out in the middle, I managed to grab a stump and it remains a very proud part of my cricket memorabilia at home, alongside my first England cap.

I was also fortunate enough to have some half-decent knocks in my time as well. I obviously look back with pride at posting two hundreds in the Test at Bridgetown in 1993/94. A bit of the gloss was removed from that in my mind as we had already lost the series, but to bounce back from the 46-all-out humiliation at Port-of-Spain in the previous Test to become the first side to defeat the West Indies in Barbados for 59 years was a great feeling, no question.

In 1992, with Mike Atherton out of action after back surgery, I quickly became Graham Gooch's regular opening partner in the series on home soil against Pakistan. I had scored four centuries in my previous five Tests – including 190 at Edgbaston – when we went to Lord's that year but weirdly, I look back almost as fondly at the half-century I posted in the second innings in a game that we lost, but which turned out to be a Lord's classic. Faced with Wasim Akram, Waqar Younis and Mushtaq Ahmed at their best, I carried my bat for 69 out of a total of 175. It was almost enough as chasing 138, Pakistan collapsed to 95 for 8, before Wasim and Waqar eventually saw them home.

It obviously wasn't a massive score on my part and I didn't bat for a huge amount of time, but to open and carry my bat through the quality of bowling of Wasim and Waqar in their prime, while everyone else at the other end seemed to be dropping like flies, means that I must have been doing something right. I guess that if we had won, I would perhaps look back on that as my proudest cricketing moment.

Having stood in for Gooch on three fruitless occasions, I was awarded the England captaincy full-time in 1998, when Mike Atherton stood down, following defeat in the Caribbean. It turned out that I had a fair bit on my plate as I carried on wicket-keeping as well through that summer's series against the South Africans. The First Test ended in a draw, and then we lost the Second Test at Lord's by ten wickets. But it was the final day of the Third Test that I look back on with very fond memories.

With South Africa having posted their highest ever score against England with 552 for five declared and then made us follow on, Mike Atherton scored 89, I scored 164 and Robert Croft held on for a crucial 37 not out as Angus Fraser blocked out the last over with the scores level and just one second innings wicket remaining. It provided us with the impetus to go on and win at Trent Bridge to level the series, and then again at Headingley in the final Test, by 23 runs. I had the pleasure of being the first England captain to win a five-Test series since Mike Gatting in 1986/87.

One of the greatest duels the game has ever seen

In that fiercely contested Test series against South Africa in 1998, the match at Trent Bridge produced the infamous Mike Atherton v. Allan Donald showdown, and to this day it remains one of the best bits of sporting drama I have ever seen. On the whole, I think it would be fair to say that cricket should not tolerate players verbally confronting one another out in the middle. But on this occasion it was another part of one of the game's all-time greatest duels.

South Africa had set us 247 to win and it must be remembered that England had not successfully chased-down a target this big in the fourth innings at home to win a match since 1902. At 82 for one everything was going smoothly until Hansie Cronje brought Donald back into the attack at the Pavilion End. Sensing that things were getting away from South Africa, Donald was clearly fired-up to try to secure a breakthrough. With the clear intention of roughing up Atherton with a few short balls, and as a new angle of attack, Donald decided to bowl round the wicket. After a fair bit of 90-mile-an-hour chin music, another short one brushed Atherton's glove and was taken by Mark Boucher behind the stumps.

As the fielders celebrated Atherton didn't go anywhere when Steve Dunne who was umpiring that day turned down the appeal. Following that and the barrage of abuse

102

he unleashed at Atherton, I reckon that his deliveries got about five- or ten-miles-an-hour faster as he continued to pepper Atherton. It was amusing to watch them stare each other out after every ball, with Atherton knowing that he would win that aspect of the contest every time because sooner or later Donald had to turn and go back to his mark for the next ball.

It was cricket – and sport as a whole – at its competitive best. I have no doubt in my mind that if you showed that to someone with no interest in sports whatsoever, they would still appreciate it and enjoy it for what it was – pure sporting theatre. And at the end of the day's play, after an hour or so of Donald trying to kill Atherton, they shared a beer together. It was exactly what sport should be about in my mind.

You win some, you lose some

Of course there are those that will think that Atherton should have walked when he gloved the ball to Boucher off Donald's bowling at Trent Bridge in 1998. Personally I disagree with that sentiment. Obviously I didn't want him to at the time, as the game still hung in the balance, but

I wouldn't expect him to now either. Early in my career I made the decision never to walk. There is no rule that says that you have to, so why do it when you are effectively surrendering your wicket? How many times does a wicket-keeper catch the ball knowing that the batsman hasn't hit it and yet he is still given out? Or more importantly, when it happens, how many times do you see a fielding side call the batsman back? The umpires are out there to make the decisions so leave it to them.

If a player wants to walk then fine, that's up to him, and equally, if he doesn't, then that's no problem either. If I'm coaching, I never tell anyone to walk. What I will say is that, if they are given out, then they shouldn't react in one particular way or another. If you've been given out and you didn't hit it then you just have to accept it – chances are the next poor decision will go in your favour. If you play cricket long enough and you're not too unlucky an individual, then it should all even itself out in the end!

I think the umpires would much prefer it if no one walked at all then they could just make a decision as they see it. The problem with it as an idea is that there are some players who try to portray themselves as walkers, and whether successful or not, this can sometimes have an effect on an umpire's decision. If they think you are a walker and then there is a big appeal and then you stand there, that might influence them into thinking that you didn't hit it. And if you are a walker and you need one run to win the Ashes and you get a feather, then are you going to stay or are you going to go?

Bruised and battered

No batsman ever walks out to the middle in the West Indies expecting an easy day at the office, but at Sabina Park, Kingston, Jamaica, on 29 January 1998 it was a different challenge altogether. They had recently relaid the pitch with a clay surface that was anything but ready to see a Test Match played on it over five days. It wasn't flat, and, right from the outset, it had a whopping great big crack all the way down it, about the width of a pen. Never mind breaking up on days four and five, it was in absolute tatters from the start.

Anyway, I opened with Mike Atherton, following him winning the toss and electing to bat. It turned out to be a fairly painful decision! Facing Curtly Ambrose and Courtney Walsh was never easy – on this pitch it was impossible. One delivery would skid past your ankles, the next – off a length – would kick up at your throat. It was ridiculous. Totally unplayable, and after only 56 minutes stumps were pulled and the game abandoned.

I had faced 26 balls and I can't remember exactly how many of those hit me and Atherton, Mark Butcher, Nasser Hussain and Graham Thorpe – who had all faced deliveries at the other end – somewhere on the body. But I can still remember the pain when I left the ground. A ground where, in 1930, Andy Sandham had hit Test cricket's first triple century, and where Gary Sobers had eclipsed it in 1958 with his brilliant unbeaten 365.

Although, after the match was officially abandoned, a further Test, in Port-of-Spain was added to the series, it was a sad day for West Indian cricket.

Sabina Park, Kingston, Jamaica

First Test:
West Indies v. England, 1930

Tests played:
West Indies – 44 (won 22, lost 9, drawn 13)
England – 15 (won 3, lost 6, drawn 6)
Australia – 10 (won 4, lost 3, drawn 3)
India – 10 (won 1, lost 6, drawn 3)
Pakistan – 3 (won 1, lost 2, drawn 0)
New Zealand – 2 (won 0, lost 1, drawn 1)
South Africa – 1 (won 0, lost 1, drawn 0)
Sri Lanka – 1 (won 0, lost 1, drawn 0)
Bangladesh – 1 (won 0, lost 1, drawn 0)
Zimbabwe – 1 (won 0, lost 1, drawn 1)

Highest innings:
England – 849 v. West Indies, 1930

Lowest innings:
West Indies – 47 all out v. England, 2004

Most runs:
Gary Sobers – 1,354 (from 11 Tests at 104.15)

Most hundreds:
Clyde Walcott – 5 (from 7 Tests)
Gary Sobers – 5 (from 11 Tests)

Most ducks:
Srinivas Venkataraghavan – 3 (in 5 innings)
Joe Solomon – 3 (in 7 innings)
Malcolm Marshall – 3 (in 10 innings)
Courtney Walsh – 3 (in 13 innings)
Chris Gayle – 3 (in 15 innings)
Brian Lara – 3 (in 20 innings)

Most wickets:
Courtney Walsh – 48 (from 11 Tests at 18.68)

Most catches:
Brian Lara – 23 (from 12 Tests)

Most Tests.
Brian Lara – 12

Most appearances as umpire:
Douglas Sang Hue – 10

66 ————————————————————

Gary Sobers was unsurpassed as an all-rounder, he always played cricket the way the Gods intended – absolutely straight, absolutely hard, but never with malice.

Trevor Bailey

———————————————————— 99

My best XI

I'm often asked to pick my best XI of all time. I can assure you, it is not an easy task. Before now I have never devoted enough time to it to commit to a list, and so have always declined. What I have always maintained, however, is that I would never commit to the best team of all time. I feel strongly that I'm only able to pass proper judgement on players that I've played with or against, and have seen over the duration of at least a major Test series. I think it is essential to have seen them in action up close, whether it be running in in full-flight, how they carry and compose themselves out in the middle, or their speed, agility and commitment in the field. All the details add up and make a real difference in my view.

Unfortunately, all of my self-imposed prerequisites don't make my job of choosing my best XI any easier …

They also have to have been playing at their peak when I played with them. In other words, I have to have witnessed, first-hand, performances that justify their selection. Not select them as a result of their reputation or performances I've either seen on television or from beyond the boundary rope.

A perfect example of this is Viv Richards. I played against Viv, but when he only had about two years of his playing career left and not in his prime. I obviously saw him as a schoolboy and then as an up-and-coming pro, and so know that he was absolutely fantastic, I just never got to play with him at his very best.

The one omission that troubles me is the brilliant Martin Crowe. He used his simple technique to great effect and it never ceased to amaze me how much time he always seemed to have to spare before the ball came onto the bat. He was a fine, fine player.

Nevertheless, I stand by my choices and so, for what it's worth, – as they would appear on the team sheet – here's my best XI (actually, I've thrown in a Twelfth Man for good measure, in case having seen the pitch I want to pick two spinners):

Best Eleven

Graham Gooch
(England, Essex)
118 Test Matches: 8,900 runs; 20 centuries; highest score 333; average 42.58; 103 catches; 23 wickets; average 46.47

126 ODIs: 4,290 runs; 8 centuries; highest score 142; average 36.98; 45 catches; 36 wickets; average 42.11

First Class: 44,846 runs; 128 centuries; highest score 333; average 49.01; 555 catches; 246 wickets; average 34.37

Matthew Hayden
(Australia, Queensland, Hampshire, Northamptonshire)
103 Test Matches: 8,625 runs; 30 centuries; highest score 380; average 50.73; 128 catches

161 ODIs: 6,133 runs; 10 centuries, highest score 181*, average 43.80; 68 catches

First Class: 24,603 runs; 79 centuries; highest score 380, average 52.57; 296 catches; 17 wickets; average 39.47

Brian Lara
(West Indies, Trinidad & Tobago, Warwickshire)
131 Test Matches: 11,953 runs; 34 centuries; highest score 400*, average 52.88; 164 catches

299 ODIs: 10,405 runs; 19 centuries; highest score 169; average 40.48; 120 catches; 4 wickets; average 15.25

First Class: 22,156 runs. 65 centuries; highest score 501*; average 51.88; 320 catches; 4 wickets; average 104.00

Sachin Tendulkar
(India, Mumbai, Yorkshire)
159 Test Matches: 12,773 runs; 42 centuries; highest score 248*; average 54.58; 102 catches; 44 wickets; average 51.63

425 ODIs: 16,684 runs; 43 centuries; highest score 186*; average 44.37; 129 catches; 154 wickets; average 44.19

First Class: 21,662 runs; 69 centuries, Highest score 248*, average 58.70; 170 catches; 69 wickets; average 60.34

Jacques Kallis
(South Africa, Western Province, Glamorgan, Middlesex)
131 Test Matches: 10,277 runs; 31 centuries; highest score 189*; average 54.66; 147 catches; 258 wickets; average 31.08

291 ODIs: 10,239 runs; 16 centuries; highest score 139; average 45.30; 105 catches; 247 wickets; average 31.90

First Class: 16,629 runs; 48 centuries, highest score 200; average 53.46; 209 catches; 393 wickets; average 30.49

Steve Waugh
(Australia, New South Wales, Kent, Somerset)
168 Test Matches: 10,927 runs; 32 centuries; highest score 200;
average 51.06; 112 catches; 92 wickets, average 37.44

325 ODIs: 7,569 runs; 3 centuries; highest score 120*; average
32.90; 111 catches; 195 wickets; average 34.67

First Class: 24,052 runs; 79 centuries; highest score 216;
average 51.94; catches 273; 249 wickets; average 32.75

Adam Gilchrist
(Australia, New South Wales, Western Australia)
96 Test Matches: 5,570 runs; 17 centuries; highest score 204*;
average 47.60; 379 catches/37 stumpings

287 ODIs: 9,619 runs; 16 centuries; highest score 172; average
35.89; 417 catches/55 stumpings

First Class: 10,334 runs, 30 centuries, highest score 204*;
average 44.16; 756 catches/55 stumpings

Wasim Akram
(Pakistan, Lahore, Hampshire, Lancashire)
104 Test Matches: 2,898 runs; 3 centuries; highest score 257*;
average 22.64; 44 catches; 414 wickets, average 23.62

356 ODIs: 3,717 runs; highest score 86; average 16.42; 88
catches; 502 wickets; average 23.52

First Class: 7,161 runs; 7 centuries; highest score 257*, average
22.73; 97 catches; 1,042 wickets; average 21.64

Shane Warne
(Australia, Victoria, Hampshire)
145 Test Matches; 3,154 runs; highest score 99; average 17.32;
125 catches; 708 wickets; average 25.41

194 ODIs: 1,018 runs; highest score 55; average 13.05;
80 catches; 293 wickets; average 25.73

First Class: 6,919 runs; 1 century, highest score 107*; average
19.43; 264 catches; 1,319 wickets; average 26.11

Curtly Ambrose
(West Indies, Leeward Islands, Northamptonshire)
98 Test Matches: 1,439 runs; highest score 53, average 12.40;
18 catches; 405 wickets; average 20.99

176 ODIs: 639 runs, highest score 31; average 10.65; 45
catches; 225 wickets; average 24.12

First Class: 3,448 runs; highest score 78; average 13.95; 88
catches; 941 wickets; average 20.24

Glenn McGrath
(Australia, New South Wales, Middlesex, Worcestershire)
124 Test Matches: 641 runs; highest score 61; average 7.36;
38 catches; 563 wickets; average 21.64

250 ODIs: 115 runs; highest score 11; average 3.83; 37 catches;
381 wickets; average 22.02

First Class: 977 runs; highest score 61; average 7.75; 54 catches;
835 wickets; average 20.85

Muttiah Muralitharan
(Sri Lanka, Kandurata, Kent, Lancashire)
127 Test Matches: 1,178 runs; highest score 67; average 11.32;
69 catches; 770 wickets; average 22.18

329 ODIs: 610 runs; highest score 33*; average 6.42; 127
catches; 505 wickets; average 22.74

First Class: 2,109 runs; highest score 67; average 11.15; 120
catches; 1,344 wickets; average 19.26

On the edge of greatness

The higher you get in sport – and particularly the game of cricket – the more you will find that the talent level equals out. Of course there will be exceptions like Tiger Woods and Donald Bradman, but on the whole, at the top, you will see pretty much a very similar level of skill on show. This is then punctuated by either great or poor performances on the pitch. The quality of these performances is obviously predominantly determined by latent talent, but there is also more to it than that. In the modern era of cut-throat professional sport, with so much riding on every game financially, there is a constant pressure to perform.

It isn't just the financial implications of hitting the winning runs or taking that final wicket. The game has changed irrevocably in so many ways as it has marched on into the twenty-first century – notably, the media involvement and all that comes with it. Of course there has always been interest from the Press in international cricket, but with so many different media outlets available in today's digital age, there seems to be more need for journalists to exaggerate and sensationalise a story in order to get it heard on the radio, seen on the TV, or bought at the news-stands. It all adds to the pressure applied to the modern cricketer, playing at the very top of the game. The simple fact is, there are players who reach that level but ultimately cannot sustain it because of everything that goes with it, and it can sometimes have a detrimental effect on their performance on the field.

In today's game, that can be the difference between an international player who gets a few caps and a great one who goes on to excel. Obviously you need the talent to get there in the first place, but then it can simply boil down to psyche, and whether a player has got the mental strength necessary to cope with everything the sport can throw at you. Some people think the idea of sport psychologists is ridiculous, on the basis that there wasn't such a thing in the game twenty years ago, so why should there be any need for them now? Well, the game has changed, it has moved on, the standard has improved and there is more at stake, and so, if a sports psychologist can make one per cent difference to a player's performance then great, use one. It's the same principle with fitness trainers and dieticians. If they help a player even slightly as a way of ensuring they can compete at the top, then there has to be a place for them in the sport.

I certainly wouldn't endorse forcing them upon a player. Everyone is different and so for some it could have a negative effect. I am all for giving people as many options as possible, but I would always want the individual to have sole responsibility for his decision making, and to use the resources around him to enable him make the correct decisions. The sports psychologist obviously can't go out and bat or bowl for you, and can't make you catch the ball, but if he can get you in a mental state so that you step onto the field in a more confident mood or a better frame of mind, then he's got to be an asset.

Sledging can also play a part. Some players respond well to it and some don't. Steve Waugh, for example, thrived on it. To such an extent that at Old Trafford in 1997 we decided not to talk to him at all when he was out in the middle. Unfortunately it didn't work as he ended up scoring centuries in both innings! However, for those players who don't like it, if they can find someone who can teach them to block it out and consequently improve their concentration, then great, why not use that?

However, there is a fine line between winding a player up – which is obviously the intention – and out-and out abuse. Thankfully it rarely stepped over to the latter in my experience and I'm not going to cite any examples I'm afraid, as I have always believed that what is said on the field stays on the field. What I will say, though, is that Merv Hughes was always pretty amusing when it came to a bit of sledging. He wasn't slow to come out with this, that and the other to build around his stock 'arsewipe', which he'd send my way after pretty much every delivery. I think it can also be safely assumed that Merv would fall into the category of players that wouldn't have requested a sports psychologist!

The media also play their very considerable part. Any player that says they don't listen to, or care, what the Press says about them is lying. Obviously some take it more to heart than others, but it all goes in and can kick around a player's mind as he's taking guard, with his Test career

– and ultimately living as well – on the line. As far as journalists are concerned, as soon as you are out of the side, you are a better player and it's your replacement's turn to have every facet of his game picked apart and found to be riddled with faults. When you win your place back, the process starts again. It's just how it is, the nature of the beast you could say, and again, some players are better at handling it than others.

As a result, all these elements have ensured that the history of the game is littered with players who didn't truly fulfil their potential and should have gone on to much greater things. Unfortunately, I witnessed a few cases first-hand. Take Mark Ramprakash and Graeme Hick for example. They are two of the most technically gifted batsmen of my era, but when all's said and done, their career figures – although obviously good – will go no way to showing how great they were:

Graeme Hick
65 Tests: 3,383 runs; 6 centuries; highest score 178; average 31.32; 90 catches; 23 wickets; average 56.78

120 ODIs: 3,846 runs; 5 centuries; highest score 126*; average 37.33; 64 catches; 30 wickets; average 34.20

First Class: 41,112 runs; 136 centuries; highest score 405*; average 52.23; 709 catches; 232 wickets; average 44.43

Mark Ramprakash
52 Tests: 2,350 runs; 2 centuries; highest score 154; average 27.32; 39 catches; 4 wickets; average 119.25

18 ODIs: 376 runs; highest score 51; average 26.85; 8 catches;
4 wickets; average 27.00

First Class: 32,064 runs; 104 centuries; highest score 301*;
average 53.52; 240 catches; 34 wickets; average 64.58

Take Stuart Law as well. Although I don't think he could be especially described as not up to the task mentally, it is just sad to see that he has not had the career a player of his quality warrants. This is particularly applicable to his Test career, where unbelievably, he only ever got one cap, against Sri Lanka in 1995, and only as a replacement for an injured Steve Waugh. In spite of him making an unbeaten 54 in his only Test innings, he was subsequently dropped upon Waugh's recovery and never played for Australia again.

He has excelled in first-class cricket throughout his career and it's obviously impossible to say if he would have gone on to great things in the Australian Test side, as he was never given the chance. Despite plying his trade in an era when there was no shortage of quality Australian batsmen, I just feel that given a decent run in the side, he would have made a place in the batting line-up his own. Anyway, having played for Essex, Lancashire and Derbyshire since 1996, he has now settled in England and taken British citizenship. He is therefore entitled to play Test cricket for England, but given the fact that he is nearly 41 years old, it seems unlikely and would be wrong.

Stuart Law

1 Test: 54 runs; highest score 54*; 1 catch

54 ODIs: 1,237 runs; 1 century; highest score 110; average 26.89; 12 catches; 12 wickets; average 52.91

First Class: 27,041 runs; 79 centuries; highest score 263; average 50.82; 79 catches; 83 wickets; average 51.03

Of course there are others that don't fulfil their potential for entirely different reasons. The death of my friend and team-mate Ben Hollioake in a car crash in March 2002 was not only a very sad day for me and all that knew him, it was a very sad day for cricket. At only 24 years old he already had two Test Matches and twenty one-day internationals under his belt, and there was absolutely no doubt that there was still much to come.

In 1997, aged only nineteen, he was called up to England's one-day international squad to play Australia. He made his debut in the third and final game of the series at Lord's and immediately displayed what the future held in store as he cracked 63 off 48 balls off a bowling attack that included Warne, Kasprowicz, Gillespie and McGrath. Some people even heralded him as the new Botham.

Although his England career had stalled in 1999–2000 (in spite of his winning the county championship with Surrey in both seasons), there were still great things to come from Ben. He would have a turned into a truly fine cricketer, and is still sorely missed within the game.

Ben Hollioake
2 Tests: 44 runs; highest score 28; average 11.00; 2 catches;
4 wickets; average 49.75

20 ODIs: 309 runs; highest score 63; average 20.60; 6 catches;
8 wickets; average 66.50

First Class: 2,794 runs; 3 centuries; highest score 163;
average 25.87; 126 wickets; average 33.45; 68 catches

Davison's bunker shot

Canada is very much a minnow of World Cup cricket. They have played in two World Cups so far, posting the record lowest scores in both. Bearing this in mind will help you realise the significance of Canada's John Davison leathering a 67-ball century against the West Indies in 2003. It was the fastest century in World Cup history, included six sixes, and came to an end only from Vasbert Drakes's catch – one of the best ever seen on a cricket field. Davison, in order to underline that his innings wasn't a fluke, then proceeded to smash a half-century against New Zealand, including a six so big that it landed on the neighbouring golf course.

Who came second?

I follow all sports but with different levels of interest and therefore different levels of knowledge. What I do know though is that I love seeing the very best of any sport performing at the top of their game. I'm also a firm believer that you only really achieve greatness if you remain at the pinnacle of your sport for a decent length of time. The term 'legend' is far too widely bandied about these days, and is too often misused to describe winners in sport that haven't set themselves apart from the rest of their field for sufficient time to warrant the accolade. A lot of people deem it boring when a sportsman gets to the top and no one can get close, but personally I admire and enjoy watching champions that can dig their heels in and make themselves the person to beat.

There are also plenty of other qualities that go towards making a great champion in my view – whether it is dignity and tenacity on the pitch, court or course, or the ability to inspire a team. I have also been fortunate enough in my time to meet some of the great champions that I admire, and so have the benefit of considering what they were like as a person away from the media-friendly public image a lot of modern-day sportsmen like to project.

Although, in order to get to the pinnacle of a sport, the chances are you have to conduct yourself as a consummate professional, it's also good to see people that can achieve that while being entertaining along the way. Take Muhammad Ali for example. He was a brilliant athlete, arguably the best heavyweight champion the world has ever seen, and yet part of his armoury, in addition to his phenomenal physical power and agility in the ring, was his ability to unsettle other boxers through talk. He was a master at getting into an opponent's head, often overtly and accurately predicting the round in which he would knock his opponent out. Anyone that can come out with 'It's hard to be humble when you're as great as I am,' then get in the ring and prove it, has to be great in my view!

I also admire people that can get themselves beyond their station with the talent they've got. In cricket this has applied to many people over the years. Take Graham Gooch for example. I worship him as a player because he used every ounce of his ability – and more – to produce what he did for Essex and England over a long period. Paul Collingwood is the same. He is not the most naturally gifted player around but he has made full use of what talent he has got and made himself a permanent part of the England set-up. His application and dedication to the game are fantastic and in a tough situation he'll guts it out for you. How many times, when England has been up against it in a Test Match, has Colly ground out a decent score to get the innings back on track? I can assure you that it is more times than people seem to remember.

I like people who you would want to go to war with you. Gooch, Collingwood and Steve Waugh are the sort of people you would want standing next to you in the trenches when you are about to go over the top. They are tough customers and when thrown into the hot cauldron of international cricket, that's what you need in a side.

Nevertheless, in the end, the simple fact is that all people in sport are judged by results. Take Avram Grant, for example. With me being an ardent Chelsea fan a lot of people asked me through his tenure as manager why he was getting such a negative reaction from the club and was ultimately sacked when, in fact, he had gone further in the Champions League than Jose Mourinho? Well, my answer is pretty simple: what silverware did he win? Nothing. I know that if John Terry hadn't slipped and put the penalty wide it would have been a very different story, but the fact is, he didn't win a trophy. You are judged on results and no one remembers who comes second. You only remember the winners and that's why I cite the following as my favourite sportsmen of all time:

Pete Sampras
Wimbledon Champion:
1993/1994/1995/1997/1998/1999/2000
US Open Champion: 1990/1993/1995/1996/2002
Australian Open Champion: 1994/1997

Roger Federer
Wimbledon Champion: 2003/2004/2005/2006/2007
US Open Champion: 2004/2005/2006/2007/2008
Australian Open Champion: 2004/2006/2007
French Open Champion: 2006/2007/2008

Tiger Woods
Open Champion: 2000/2005/2006
US Open Champion: 2000/2002/2008
PGA Championship: 1999/2000/2006/2007
The Masters: 1997/2001/2002/2005

Michael Johnson
Olympic Games Gold Medal: 200m 1996; 400m 1996/2000;
4×4 400m Relay 1992
World Championships Gold Medal: 200m 1991/1995; 400m
1993/1995/1997/1999; 4×4 400m Relay 1993/1995/1999

Steve Redgrave
Olympic Games Gold Medal: Coxed Four 1984; Coxless Pair
1988/1992/1996/2000
World Championships Gold Medal: Coxed Pair 1986;
Coxless Pair 1987/1991/1993/1994/1995; Coxless Four
1997/1998/1999
Commonwealth Games Gold Medal: Single Sculls 1986;
Coxless Pair 1986; Coxed Four 1986
Knighted in 2001

Muhammad Ali
World Heavyweight Champion: 1964–67 and 1974–78

Gianfranco Zola
Honours with Parma: UEFA Super Cup 1993 and UEFA Cup
1995
Honours with Chelsea: UEFA Cup Winners Cup 1998; UEFA
Super Cup 1998
FA Cup: 1997/2000
FA Charity Shield: 2000

Coca-Cola Cup: 1998
FWA Footballer of the Year: 1997
OBE: 2004
English Football Hall of Fame: 2006
International caps: 35 for Italy, 10 goals

Alan Shearer
Honours with Blackburn Rovers: Premier League 1994/95
FWA Player of the Year: 1994
PFA Players Player of the Year: 1995, 1997
English Football Hall of Fame: 2004
International caps: 63 for England, 30 goals

'Sugar' Ray Leonard
Olympic Games Gold Medal: Light Welterweight 1976
World Welterweight Champion: 1979
World Light Middleweight Champion: 1981
World Middleweight Champion: 1987
World Super Middleweight Champion: 1988
World Light Heavyweight Champion: 1988

Lance Armstrong
World Cycling Champion: 1993
Tour de France Winner:
1999/2000/2001/2002/2003/2004/2005

Rise from the Ashes

The 1981 series – or 'Botham's Ashes' as it came to be known – saw probably the greatest comeback in Test history. At Headingley, in the Third Test, England were made to follow on, being 227 runs behind. Famously, an English bookmaker offered odds of 500-1 for an English victory, upon which Australian players Dennis Lillee and Rod Marsh peculiarly laid a small bet. England, reduced to 135 for seven in their second innings, looked like they were heading for a crushing defeat. Instead, they put on 221 for the last three wickets, Botham finishing on an unbeaten 149 and leaving Australia 130 to chase. A piece of cake for a team which was already leading the series 1-0, most would have thought. The Australians weren't counting on Willis taking eight for 43, however, and they were dismissed for 111, giving England a miraculous victory by eighteen runs. Lillee and Marsh might have won some money, but that was scant consolation for the pain inflicted by such a defeat.

‟

A Test Match without Botham is like a horror film without Boris Karloff.

Fred Trueman

„

The fastest growing sport in the world

Women's cricket in this country goes from strength to strength. The England side has recently returned triumphantly from Australia with the World Cup in their possession, having beaten New Zealand by four wickets in the final at the North Sydney Oval. They lost only one match in the tournament, against Australia, while they defeated India, Pakistan, New Zealand, Sri Lanka and the West Indies, with five England players named in the composite ICC team of the tournament.

In spite of being written off as serious underdogs prior to the tour of Australia in 2008, England drew the one-day international series and also successfully retained the Ashes, having won them in 2005 for the first time in 42 years. In the 2005 World Cup, England lost in the semi-finals, but to eventual winners Australia.

Basically, women's cricket in England is in a very healthy state indeed – and thriving. This is embodied by the fact that Claire Taylor – the leading run-scorer in the 2009 World Cup – has just been named as one of *Wisden*'s Five Cricketers of the Year. She is the first woman ever to receive the accolade, since *Wisden* introduced the annual roll of honour in 1889, 120 years ago.

Scyld Berry, the editor of *Wisden Cricketers' Almanack*, explained the reason for her inclusion among England bowler James Anderson, Durham's Dale Benkenstein and the South Africans Mark Boucher and Neil McKenzie:

> 'Beating Australia in Australia is the objective for all cricketers, at least in England, and Claire almost single-handedly saw England through to victory and the retention of the Ashes in Australia last year, not to mention her success in the World Cup just a couple of weeks back. It would be a sin of omission, an act of prejudice, to exclude her from the accolade.
>
> 'The England women have been the pride of the nation as far as cricket is concerned in recent years, and Claire's nomination as a Cricketer of the Year is testament to the sterling effort the ladies have consistently put in.
>
> 'James Anderson has been England's most reliable pace bowler in the last year; Dale Benkenstein guided Durham to their first Championship, while Mark Boucher and Neil McKenzie were the backbone of the South African side that defeated England last summer.'

It's a formidable list of cricketers, but no one can deny Claire's right to be included. Some people argue that fewer women play cricket than men, so the consequent anomaly in standard means that men's and women's games should never be compared for anything like this. Well, I say that you can only play what's put in front of you and Claire has done that consistently at the very top of her game for a long time now, and so justly deserves the recognition.

Someone told me recently that women's cricket is the fastest growing sport in the world. I have to say that I didn't know that but I was pleasantly surprised. I think it's great and will be self-perpetuating as well – the more people that play a sport, the higher the skill levels inevitably become. As the standard goes up so does the competition for places in the top international sides, and with competition comes the need for further improvement. As well as that, I love the game of cricket so the more people that play it, at any age, nationality or sex across the world, the better.

Women's Cricket

First recorded women's cricket match:
'Eleven maids of Bramley versus eleven maids of Hambledon'
at Godsden Common, near Guildford, Surrey, 1745

First Test Match:
Australia v. England, 1934

First Test Match in England:
England v. Australia at Northampton, 1937

First match at Lord's:
(ODI) England v. Australia, 1976

Tests played:
England – 87 (won 19, lost 11, drawn 57)
Australia – 67 (won 18, lost 9, drawn 40)
New Zealand – 45 (won 2, lost 10, drawn 33)
West Indies – 12 (won 1, lost 3, drawn 8)
South Africa – 11 (won 1, lost 4, drawn 6)
Pakistan – 3 (won 0, lost 2, drawn 1)
Ireland – 1 (won 1, lost 0, drawn 0)
Sri Lanka – 1 (won 1, lost 0, drawn 0)
Netherlands – 1 (won 0, lost 1, drawn 0)

Highest innings:
Australia – 569 for 6 declared v. England, 1998

Lowest innings:
England – 35 all out v. Australia, 1958

Most runs:
Janette Brittin (England) – 1935 (from 27 Tests at 49.61)

Most hundreds:
Janette Brittin (England) – 5 (from 27 Tests)

Most ducks:
Lucy Pearson (England) – 6 (in 14 innings)

Most wickets:
Mary Duggan (England) – 77 wickets (from 17 Tests at 13.49)

Most catches:
Carole Hodges (England) – 25 (from 18 Tests)

Most Tests:
Janette Brittin (England) 27

England v. Australia

16 Test series since 1934–35
(Ashes Trophy created 1998)

Australia won 6
England won 4
Drawn 6

Ashes Trophy last won by England in Australia in 2007/08

Ashes Trophy series record since 1998 – England and Australia
have both won a series twice and 1 series has been drawn

ODI World Cup Competitions and host country:

England – 1973 and 1993
India – 1977/78 and 1997/98
New Zealand – 1981/82 and 2000/01
Australia – 1988/89 and 2008/09
South Africa – 2004/05

Australia won 5
England won 3 (including 2008/09)
New Zealand won 1

England captain Claire Taylor named as first woman 'Wisden
Cricketer of the Year' in 2009.

"

This is very exciting for cricket as a sport. Half the nation are female, and we're actually beginning to take advantage of that, and not just ask them to make tea.

Giles Clarke, ponders the glory of England women's
World Cup victory 24 March 2009

"

Low-key genius

In the Old Trafford Test in 1956, Jim Laker bowled 68 of England's 191 overs in the match. With it, he took nineteen of the twenty possible Australian wickets – a record that probably will never be surpassed.

Driving himself back to Surrey after the game, he stopped for a sandwich and a beer in a pub on the way. Customers were watching repeats of his performance on a TV, so he joined them to watch but went unrecognised. Once he was done, he quietly left, no one realising whose company they had just been in.

In a few years time, we'll wonder what all the fuss was about

I know that he had already used it against Murali the previous summer, but when Kevin Pietersen used the switch hit properly for the first time on 17 June 2008 in a one-day international against New Zealand, the game changed forever. That might sound a little dramatic but the fact he used it twice in the game and both of experienced medium-pacer Scott Styris's deliveries were dispatched over cover for six, meant that the game immediately had a new shot.

I was surprised and disappointed to hear former players like Richard Hadlee and Michael Holding complaining about it as a shot. It's an extremely high-risk thing for a batsman to do, so to say that it puts the bowler at a serious disadvantage is wrong in my view. It's just another shot for a batsman to add to his selection and another sign that the game is evolving and moving on, which I'm all for. The reverse sweep also got its fair share of stick when people started to use it back in the 1970s and now it's a part of the coaching method and an established part of the game. That's why I was very pleased to see that the MCC didn't succumb to pressures coming from certain quarters calling for the shot to be banned.

"

This idea that umpires are always right is a load of old cobblers. What I want to know is: who umpires the umpires? The players suffer from their mistakes, but no one ever seems to get rid of the umpires themselves. Being an umpire is a people job: that's why Dickie Bird was good at it. Yes, he was a loony, and he made mistakes – everyone does. But he knew how to deal with people, so they respected him.

Geoff Boycott

"

The jury's out

Umpiring is the hardest job in world cricket. No question. Of course, the performances of both players and umpires are scrutinised with a microscope these days, but there is a very considerable difference. If a batsman makes a howling error then the chances are, a couple of minutes later, he is back in the pavilion removing his pads; and if a bowler begins to bowl loosely, the chances are the captain will bring his spell to an end. Basically, they will both be removed from the spotlight, whereas an umpire is out there in the middle dealing with the intensity of professional cricket for the entire match. If an umpire makes a howler of a decision then it will be brutally exposed by technology and there is nowhere to go.

I'm not condoning poor umpiring decisions, far from it, but a simple fact of human nature is that none of us is perfect and we all make mistakes. Of course, there are some that make more mistakes than others, but on the whole I have a huge respect for umpires. The best of the lot, as far as I was concerned, was David Shepherd. Not only was his decision-making excellent, he was firm, so he earned the respect of the players, which is hugely important when you need to officiate a match with people's careers on the line. Of the current crop – and with similar qualities as Shep – is Simon Taufel, who I think is excellent. His standard of umpiring is something that some of the other umpires on the international circuit should aspire to. At international level you have the best players so you should have the best umpires as well. If you don't perform as a player then you get dropped, and the same principle should apply for umpires – make too many mistakes, they get dropped as well.

This can, in part, be regulated by the new referral system that was first tried in the 2002 Champions Trophy, then in the 2005 Super Series, and which now seems to be making its way into the game permanently. But a lot of people are against it. Personally, I'm all for it. As with everything in life, you strive for perfection, and if the referral system eradicates – or corrects – some mistakes made by umpires and gets decision-making closer to perfection, then that has to be a good thing. In trials so far the correct decision has gone up from 93 to 98 per cent, which kind of proves the point. No one is trying to undermine umpires or make them redundant, you are simply giving them as much assistance as possible in order to ensure that, ultimately, the correct decision is reached. But I do question why it is still being trialled and revised at Test level. That aspect of it seems crazy to me. In essence it's a great idea, but the ICC should have tested it properly in other forms of the game across the world, ironed out any issues that have surfaced and ensured it was ready for the highest echelon of the game. I would have the umpires referring their decisions and not the players though.

The long-term upside is that it will also bring a higher level of honesty into the game. Because the stakes are so high, very few people walk anymore. However, you are not going to say that you didn't hit it if you know that you're going to be shown up and have wasted a referral. The same applies with the bowling side. Some teams will appeal at anything and everything, a lot of the time knowing full well that it's not even close to being a wicket. Are they going to ask for a referral even though they don't think that he's hit it? 'No' is the answer, and so it enforces more sportsmanship within the game because, ironically, although the system increases the presence of another official, it also ensures that it's more player-regulated.

At the moment the third umpire is often called upon to adjudicate on a run-out decision. It takes time for it to be referred up to his room, for him to watch the replay on television and then relay the decision back to the middle. But that is fine as a wicket – and therefore a very important moment in the game – hangs in the balance. The third umpire is also sometimes needed to adjudicate whether a sliding fielder has managed to stop a ball from hitting the boundary rope or not. When all said and done, this can take nearly two minutes and we're talking about the difference between two runs, maybe only one, if the batsmen have already run three. The point being, this is time invested in a moment that doesn't normally have much effect on a match (obviously there are exceptions to the rule – see *When two runs can make the world of difference* on page 138). If someone is given out lbw when the ball has pitched outside leg stump, then it is far more likely to change the course of a game. So if the referral system can help address the more important decisions as well, then that can only be good for the game.

Catches and whether the ball has carried or not can often be a grey area. Television is only two-dimensional and often doesn't tell the whole story. That's why so many players still stand their ground, because a batsman will always be given the benefit of the doubt, so they know they would get away with it. I noticed that several players – notably Graeme Smith following their Test series with Australia in South Africa – have questioned the point in using technology, but not Hawkeye when it's readily available. Personally I wouldn't use Hawkeye in order to determine whether the ball is going to hit the stumps or not, as it's not 100 per cent foolproof. We should only use certain aspects of technology when we know that it is completely reliable and will categorically remove any chances of human error. If the technology can't do that, then don't use it until it can.

I don't think that umpires should see the referral system as a negative. They should accept that we can all make wrong decisions and therefore regard it as an aid. More often than not, a referral will, in fact, show that an umpire has made the correct decision, so he should see that as public endorsement of the good job he's doing, and not the other way around. Some people have tried to put a spin on the system so that it is solely regarded as a way of exposing the inadequacies of umpires, and that just isn't right.

People joke about what some of the old school and outspoken umpires like Dickie Bird would have made of it, if it had been introduced in his day, but like all things in cricket, however ardently we feel about sticking with a particular aspect of the game, we should move with the times and consider all options. You could ask what Sir Alec Bedser – the master of consistent line and length and hitting the seam – would have made of Twenty20. Deliveries of his that more often than not would have been left to go through to the wicket-keeper or tentatively prodded outside off stump to cover point are now disappearing out of the ground over square leg. It's just a sign of the times and how the game has moved on. The same applies to other sports as well. Having said that, if, ultimately, we discover that the referral system is too flawed, then we must be prepared to admit we got it wrong, remove it from the game and move on. Just don't ever stand still.

When two runs can make the world of difference

In the 1987 World Cup, Australia played India in their opening game. Australia batted first and at one point during their innings, Aussie No. 3 Dean Jones hit Maninder Singh for what the batsman thought was a six.

Umpire Dickie Bird was unsure and so – prior to the usage of the third umpire – asked Ravi Shastri, who was fielding on the boundary and who said it was only a four. Dickie Bird took his word for it and so awarded a four.

The Aussies complained about the decision after their innings, having seen the replay on television. In response, Dickie Bird asked Ravi Shastri again, who this time admitted that it might have cleared the boundary rope for a six.

The Australian total was adjusted from 269 to 271, which turned out to be fairly important, as the team ended up winning the match by one run!

I'm not here to make friends

In 1930 Australia toured England and won the Ashes with the brilliant Don Bradman scoring a ridiculous 974 runs across the series, a record that still remains today. Subsequently in 1932, England captain Douglas Jardine devised a tactic that came to be known as 'Bodyline'. His fast bowlers would aim at the bodies of Australian batsmen in the hope that, while trying to defend themselves, they would provide relatively simple catches to the large number of fielders he had placed close in on the leg side. Successful as it was in that it halved Bradman's batting average and ensured that England won the Ashes, it also badly injured a number of other Australian batsmen and ultimately caused a full-on diplomatic crisis.

While Bradman did his best to counter 'Bodyline' by stepping to the leg side and cutting the ball to the vacant off-side field (and was hit above the waist only once throughout the series), some of his team-mates fared rather worse. Things came to a head in Adelaide in the Third Test, when English fast bowler Harold Larwood fractured Bert Oldfield's skull and hit Australian captain Bill Woodfull in the chest, just above the heart. When Jardine placed his fielders in 'Bodyline' positions after Woodfull's injury there was almost a riot in the ground, with police having to protect the English players from the enraged spectators. 'I've not travelled 6,000 miles to make friends. I'm here to win the Ashes,' was Jardine's later response.

In 2004, in a poll of cricket journalists, commentators and players, the 'Bodyline' Series was ranked the most important event in cricket history.

> *Were cricket and football abolished, it would bring upon the masses nothing but misery, depression, sloth, indiscipline and disorder.*
>
> Lord Birkenhead

A sorry sign of the times

A sorry sign of the times is the fact that the MCC and ECB have been considering introducing yellow cards into minor county and club cricket. They have also indicated that if the system is brought in and proves a success then it is also likely to be extended to first-class cricket in the future. I'm all for competitive sport and most of what the competitive angle brings, but the fact that the governing bodies have felt the need to implement this is a sad indictment of the grass roots of the game in this country. Unfortunately, their thinking is justified as well. I'm not talking about county cricket and beyond, where you rarely see behaviour that would warrant the issuing of a yellow card. It seems that the higher the level, the more a player respects the game and the umpire. I still watch club cricket however, and sometimes behaviour levels are poor.

What a lot of these idiots need to remember is that without umpires – whether good, bad or indifferent – you don't have a game. Without them, the players might as well go home because a competitive game can't be staged. And how long are umpires going to continue to give up their evenings and weekends to officiate a game – that they no doubt love – when the reality is that week after week they are being shown little or no respect by the people on the pitch? The answer is 'not very long' and with a shortage of umpires, the whole club cricket network would implode.

So if the reality is that umpires need the yellow card as a tool to help retain the necessary level of discipline in the game then we will just have to accept it as a sad sign of the times and see if it works. But like all new policies introduced into a sport, it will need working out and trialling. A rugby player is sin-binned for ten minutes, so why can't a cricketer be made to leave the field for twelve overs? Time will tell and let's just hope that discipline – or a lack of it – doesn't destroy grassroots cricket in the same way that it is destroying football, which is currently losing over 7,000 referees a year.

Running the game we all love

– Cricket Official Bodies –

ICC (International Cricket Council)

1909
Founded as the Imperial Cricket Conference by England,
Australia and South Africa (administered by MCC from
Lord's)

1926
New members: India, New Zealand and West Indies

1952
New member: Pakistan

1961
South Africa loses membership

1965
ICC renamed International Cricket Conference (ICC)

1989
ICC renamed International Cricket Council (ICC)

1981
New member: Sri Lanka

1991
South Africa re-elected

1992
New member: Zimbabwe

1993
ICC no longer administered by MCC (HQ remains at Lord's)

2000
New member: Bangladesh

2005
ICC moves HQ from Lord's to Dubai

Responsible for managing the playing conditions and the Code of Conduct for international fixtures; organising the major international tournaments, including the World Cup.

10 Full Members
34 Associate Members
60 Affiliate Members

ECB (England and Wales Cricket Board)

Responsible since 1997 for administration of professional and recreational cricket in England and Wales.

The Marylebone Cricket Club

Guardian of the Laws of Cricket

PCA (Professional Cricketers' Association)

Formed in 1967 (as the Cricketers' Association)

Provides financial, legal and benevolent assistance for current and past professional cricketers.

FICA (Federation of International cricketers' Associations)

Established in 1968 to co-ordinate and protect the interests of professional cricketers throughout the world.

"

I'd have looked even faster in colour.

Fred Trueman

"

The Cricket World Cup in stats and facts

- There have been 9 World Cup Tournaments between 1975 and 2007
  Winners: 4 Australia, 2 West Indies, 1 India, Pakistan, Sri Lanka.

- The highest team total in the World Cup: 413 for 5 (50.0 overs) – India v. Bermuda 2006/07.

- The lowest team total in the World Cup: 36 (18.4 overs) – Canada v. Sri Lanka 2003.

- After Australia beat New Zealand in the 1987 World
  Cup, the Aussies got up at 6am the following day to
  train on the front lawn of their hotel – so the Kiwis
  would see them as they boarded the coach to the
  airport.

- The strike rate (the average number of runs per
  100 balls faced) for South African Lance Klusener
  from his eleven World Cup innings is 121.17
  – better than any other batsman to have graced the
  tournament in its history. He also has the highest
  batting average in any World Cup, with 140.5 in 1999.

- In 1996, South Africa's Gary Kirsten hammered an
  unbeaten 188 runs from a hapless bowling attack
  from the United Arab Emirates. It remains the Cricket
  World Cup's highest individual score.

- India's Sachin Tendulkar has scored 1,796 (average
  57.93) runs in the World Cup – more than any other
  player.

- Most hundreds: 4, Sourav Ganguly (India), Ricky
  Ponting (Australia), Sachin Tendulkar (India), Mark
  Waugh (Australia).

- The fastest delivery ever recorded was bowled in
  a preliminary group match between Pakistan and
  England in the 2003 World Cup. Pakistan's Shoaib
  Akhtar fired the ball down at the unfortunate Nick
  Knight at 100.2 mph (161.3 km/h)!

- Australia's Glenn McGrath has taken 71 wickets (average 18.19) in the World Cup – more than any other player. He has also taken most wickets in a Tournament – 26 in 2006/07.

- In the first-ever World Cup cricket match on 7 June 1975, the great Indian opening batsman Sunil Gavaskar batted through his country's entire 60-over innings for just 36 runs. It would probably be fair to say that the Indian side hadn't really got the idea behind one-day cricket at that point. Chasing England's 334, they managed just 132 but still had seven wickets in hand at the end of their innings.

- In 1983, India's Kapil Dev hit an unbeaten 175 against Zimbabwe in what was one of the all-time great World Cup innings. However, it was lost to posterity as the BBC had gone on strike that day, so there's no footage of it whatsoever.

- In 1996, Javed Miandad became the first and only player to have taken part in all six World Cups up to that point.

- India has a 100 per cent record against Pakistan in the Cricket World Cup.

- At 21 years and 75 days, Australia's Ricky Ponting was the youngest player to score a World Cup century – an unbeaten record. He has also taken more catches as a fielder than any other player, with 25.

- Best bowling figures in a World Cup match: 7 for 15 – Australia's Glenn McGrath v. Namibia in 2003.

- Best bowling economy rate in the World Cup (qualification 1,000 balls): 3.24 Andy Roberts for West Indies.

- Best bowling strike rate in the World Cup (qualification 1,000 balls): 27.50 Glenn McGrath for Australia.

- Namibian bowling all-rounder Rudi van Vuuren played in the 2003 Cricket World Cup. Nothing particularly amazing about that, you might think, except that he also represented his country in the Rugby World Cup later that year.

- When Sri Lanka played Bangladesh in 2003, Chaminda Vaas made World Cup history by taking three wickets with the very first three balls of the game. As if that wasn't enough, he got his fourth by the end of the over, leaving Bangladesh on 5 for 4 and well on their way to a ten-wicket defeat. Vaas went on to be the tournament's leading wicket-taker.

- Other hat-tricks: Chetan Sharma, India v. New Zealand, 1987/88; Saqlain Mushtaq, Pakistan v. Zimbabwe, 1999; Brett Lee, Australia v. Kenya, 2002/03.

- Four wickets in four balls – Lasith Malinga for Sri Lanka v. South Africa 2006/07.

- In the 1979 final, Viv Richards walked out to the crease with the West Indies on 22. Several hours later he returned to the pavilion on 138 not out, having just dispatched the last ball into the Mound Stand for six to set England a target of 287 to win the World Cup. In spite of Mike Brearley and Geoff Boycott getting off to a slow start, England seemed to be just about on target until they collapsed from 183 for 2 to 194 all out, with West Indian paceman Joel Garner taking five wickets in just eleven balls.

- When the West Indies played Sri Lanka in 2003, Ramnaresh Sarwan scored 47. Now that may not seem like a particularly big score, but in order to complete his innings, Sarwan had to discharge himself from hospital. Early in his innings, he was hit on the head by a bouncer and rushed to A & E. In spite of medical advice to the contrary, Sarwan hastily returned to the ground and steered his side to within a whisker of an unlikely victory.

- Most runs in a Tournament: 673 Sachin Tendulkar (India) 2002/03.

- Highest partnership for any wicket: 318 (second) Sourav Ganguly and Rahul Dravid for India v. Sri Lanka 1999.

- Most dismissals by a wicket-keeper: 52 (45 caught/ 7 stumped) Adam Gilchrist (Australia).

- Most dismissals by a wicket-keeper in an innings: 6 (all caught) Adam Gilchrist for Australia v. Namibia 2002/03.

- Most dismissals by a wicket-keeper in a Tournament: 21 by Adam Gilchrist (Australia) 2002/03.

- Most appearances in World Cup matches: 39 by Glenn McGrath and Ricky Ponting for Australia.

"

Playing against a team with Ian Chappell as captain turns a cricket match into gang warfare.

Mike Brearley

"

'You guys are history'

These are the immortal words uttered to a chortling slip cordon by Devon Malcolm at The Oval in August 1994 in the Third Test upon being hit on the head by a bouncer from South Africa's Fanie de Villiers.

What followed was the fastest spell I've ever seen from an England bowler. Devon's retribution was swift and brutal, tearing through openers Peter and Gary Kirsten, before dispatching Hansie Cronje to reduce South Africa to 1-3. I remember he got Peter Kirsten caught on the boundary with a top edge by Phil De Freitas and from that moment on nobody took him on for the hook shot. He went on to destroy the South African batting line-up in their second innings with figures of nine for 57: the third-best Test bowling figures by an Englishman, surpassed only by Jim Laker's ten for 53 and nine for 37 at Old Trafford in 1956.

At the time it was the sixth-best bowling figures in Test history and it set us up for an eight-wicket victory to see us level the series. It was a great, great performance and one that, as a fielder, it was a pleasure to watch. I wasn't keeping wicket that day but fielding at cover and slip, so could witness the pace from differing angles. Trust me when I tell you that he was rapid that day. Mind you, Devon always had genuine pace, it's just that his radars were very much in the right place that day and he was fiercely consistent as well.

The Oval crowd also played their part. They were fantastic and got behind Devon and roared him on from the start, following those quick early wickets. When asked in the past what I thought was the best spell I ever kept wicket to, I've always said that it was Andrew Caddick against the West Indies at Lord's in 2000 when he took five for sixteen in their second innings. Well, I wasn't keeping wicket for Devon's spell that day but I can still safely say that it was right up there.

The Top 10 Best Figures in a Test Innings:

Jim Laker – 10 for 53, England v. Australia, 1956
Anil Kumble – 10 for 74, India v. Pakistan, 1999
George Lohmann – 9 for 27, England v. South Africa, 1896
Jim Laker – 9 for 37, England v. Australia, 1956
Muttiah Muralitharan – 9 for 51, Sri Lanka v. Zimbabwe, 2002
Richard Hadlee – 9 for 52, New Zealand v. Australia, 1985
Abdul Qadir – 9 for 56, Pakistan v. England, 1987
Devon Malcolm – 9 for 57, England v. South Africa, 1994
Muttiah Muralitharan – 9 for 65, Sri Lanka v. England, 1998

Cricket – a game which the English, not being a spiritual people, have invented in order to give themselves some conception of eternity.

Lord Mancroft

Black holes and purple patches

If Ray Illingworth had had his way, my career would probably have ended in his clearout following our defeat in the Test series in South Africa in 1995/96. I was dropped for the First Test of the summer against India, but earned a recall for the Second Test at Lord's when my replacement, Nick Knight, broke a finger. I top-scored in the second innings with 66 and then never looked back, scoring 3 centuries and 6 half-centuries in my next eight matches.

Two of those hundreds came in back-to-back Tests in Zimbabwe and New Zealand, and, for the first time, they were posted when I was also in charge of wicket-keeping duties. After scoring an unbeaten 101 in the drawn Test at Harare, I knocked up 173 at Auckland, the highest score ever recorded by an England wicket-keeper. I had been handed back the keeper's gloves at the end of the previous summer after scoring 170 against Pakistan at Headingley.

This isn't an exercise for me to rattle off a series of good scores I had in a particular purple patch of my career in order to make myself look good. The point I'm trying to make is that – like in any sport – players have high points, but for every good run of form the chances are there is a poor one lurking just around the corner. Or conversely, if you are a quality batsman then for every black hole, a purple patch lies in wait. It is just up to the selectors as to whether they have the trust to see that player's quality shines through, given sufficient chance.

If you are a good player with a track record behind you and you are going through a bad patch, you stay in the side longer because you have a track record for the selectors who are backing you, to say that you will come good again. Whereas, if you are just starting off and you don't perform you get left out, as they've got nothing to fall back on to say you've done it before. That's why the continuity of selection that's now in the England team is much better, as it allows new players to settle in. Whereas, when I was playing in the early 1990s, if you had one bad game it was 'see you later' – and perhaps you weren't seen again. So, from that point of view, nowadays it's easier to establish or re-establish yourself within a team than it would have been in the past.

Some of the greatest names in the history of the game have suffered some horror patches when they could not post a score. The sign of a good player is how they deal with adversity: when it gets tough they bounce back.

The Highs and the Lows

A record five hundreds in consecutive Test Match innings

Everton Weekes

Weekes scored 141 for West Indies against England at Kingston in March 1948. His next Test Match was 9 months later when he completed 128 against India at Delhi. This was immediately followed by 194 at Bombay and then hundreds in both innings at Calcutta.

The record could have been increased to six if he had not been run out for 90 in his next innings at Madras.

A record six hundreds in consecutive Test Matches

Don Bradman

In the 1936/37 Ashes series in Australia Bradman scored 270 in the Third Test, 212 in the fourth and 169 in the fifth. When Australia toured England in 1938 he began with 144 not out at Trent Bridge followed by an unbeaten 102 at Lord's. The Third Test was abandoned without a ball being bowled and the record came with 103 at Headingley

Due to injury Bradman was unable to bat in the Fifth Test at The Oval but scored 187 and 234 in his next two Test Matches in the 1946/47 series.

A record six hundreds in consecutive first-class innings

C.B. Fry

1901 was a good year for Fry. By the end of July he had already scored seven centuries. On 15 August he added another, with 106 for Sussex against Hampshire and then continued to pile up the centuries every time he went to the wicket against the counties Yorkshire, Middlesex, Surrey and Kent. He ended his season at Lord's in September, playing for The Rest against the champion county Yorkshire and scored his sixth consecutive hundred, his thirteenth of the season.

1,000 runs in May

W.G. Grace

When the Benefit match for Walter Read at The Oval ended on 28 May 1895, Grace had scored 847 runs since the ninth of the month, including two double centuries against Somerset and Kent. He now had only two days of the match for Gloucestershire against Middlesex to make a further 153 runs and become the first player ever to make 1,000 runs in the first month of the season.

A large crowd turned up at Lord's to see Grace win the toss and start batting immediately. Before the end of the afternoon he was receiving a standing ovation as he walked back into the pavilion after being bowled for 169 and the target reached with 1,016 runs at an average of 112.89.

W.G. was delighted with what he saw as the pinnacle of his career – 'The feat had never been achieved before, and it was naturally a matter of supreme satisfaction to me that I should, in my forty-seventh year, be enabled to surpass all the achievements of my youth.'

Only two players have scored 1,000 runs in May since: Wally Hammond in 1927 and Charlie Hallows in 1928.

Most runs in a calendar month

Len Hutton

On 1 June 1949 Hutton scored an unbeaten 146 for Yorkshire against Scotland at Hull. A double century against Lancashire and 104 and 76 against Northamptonshire was followed by 101 for England against New Zealand in a Test Match at Headingley. An unexpected trio of ducks came next but Hutton was soon scoring runs again with a century against Middlesex and a brace of hundreds at Hove against Sussex. When the month of June ended Hutton had reached a record 1,294 runs with an average of 92.43.

Back from the dead

Denis Compton

After scoring 202 for Middlesex against Cambridge University at Fenner's on 6 June 1946 Compton's next five innings were 0, 0, 0, 8 and 1. Going in at the fall of the first wicket for England against India at Lord's on 22 June, he was bowled first ball for another duck, his fourth in six trips to the wicket.

Unfazed by his shocking loss of form, two days after the end of the Test, Compton returned to Lord's and scored 122 against Warwickshire. He ended the season as leading scorer with 2,403 runs, 10 hundreds and an average of 61.61.

Ignore the critics and believe in yourself

Mark Taylor

Taylor had not reached 50 in 21 previous Test Match innings when he walked out to open the second innings for Australia against England at Edgbaston in 1997. Since the 1996/97 winter he had scraped together 367 runs with an average of 18.35 and stubbornly ignored loud and persistent demands that he resign the captaincy and withdraw from the team.

Putting the past behind him, Taylor scored 129 and went on to play in another 22 Test Matches to end his career with a total of 7,525 runs, 19 hundreds and an average of 43.40, plus a record as one of Australia's most successful captains.

Stuck on 99

Mark Ramprakash

Before the start of the 2008 English season Mark Ramprakash had already scored 97 hundreds and it seemed only a matter of time before he would join the other 24 players who had reached the coveted one hundred centuries in first-class cricket.

It took a little longer than many, including Mark himself, had probably expected.

The season began well enough with a couple of hundreds by 3 May but these were followed by 10 innings in which he failed to reach a half-century let alone the all-important three figures. The first five of those innings produced only 86 runs and the next two in June only 63. July saw no improvement and began with 48 runs from three innings. When Surrey began their second innings against Yorkshire at Headingley, Ramprakash averaged only 20.70 from the previous 10 innings but the waiting was over and an unbeaten 112 finally brought membership of that exclusive club of centurions. With the pressure off, he began adding more hundreds to his record with 200 against Somerset, 178 against Sussex and 127 against Kent before the season ended.

A captain struggles but comes out on top

Nasser Hussain

In the summer of 2000 England celebrated winning a series against West Indies for the first time after 31 years. The success had been plotted and planned by the new partnership between captain and coach, Nasser Hussain and Duncan Fletcher, who had joined forces only a few months earlier during the winter tour of South Africa.

While the England squad enjoyed this revival to their fortunes, their captain was suffering a depressing loss of personal form with the bat. Losing the First Test by an innings, Hussain had managed to score only fifteen and eight going in first-wicket down. A broken thumb put him out of the Second Test at Lord's, where I stood in as captain and we secured a narrow but well deserved victory. Hussain was back in charge for the drawn Third Test but only reached ten in the first innings and was six not out when the game ended with England 213 runs short of another win with nine wickets in hand. England crushed the West Indies at Leeds in the next Test by an innings and 39 runs in only the seventh Test to be completed within two days since 1900. For a short while it seemed that Hussain was back to form when sharing a third wicket stand of 70 runs with Thorpe, but the captain was the first to go with only 22 to his name.

So the scene was set for the conclusion to a memorable series for England at The Oval. Thanks to some determined batting from Man-of-the-Match Mike Atherton, who top-scored in both innings with 83 and 108 after more than twelve hours in the middle, England won by 158 runs. Hussain's contribution was 0 and 0 and a grand total for the series of 61 runs, with an average of 10.16. But never at any time had Hussain allowed his own dismal form to affect his responsibilities as captain, and he could take pleasure from the outstanding efforts of his players, which brought success to them all as a team under his leadership.

They thought it was all over

Sachin Tendulkar

A century in the first innings at Delhi against Sri Lanka on 10 December 2005 and it looked like business-as-usual for the 'Little Master' who had already scored over 10,000 Test runs with 35 hundreds and an average over 50 since his debut in 1989.

But the next time Tendulkar reached three figures would be almost eighteen months in the future. He contributed only another 58 runs in his next three innings against Sri Lanka, and when India went to Pakistan at the beginning of 2006 he managed only 63 runs from another three innings. At the end of the series the front page of *The Times of India* carried the headline – 'ENDULKAR?'

England arrived in India next and Tendulkar continued to struggle with only 83 runs from five innings and was even booed in the Third Test in his home town of Mumbai after being dismissed for a single, leaving India at 28 for three. Since the 109 at Delhi, he had only scored 204 runs from eleven innings, with an average of 20.40. The runs slowly began to return during India's tour of South Africa, posting 199 from six innings at 33.17, before Tendulkar took advantage of a series against Bangladesh in May 2007 to start scoring centuries again – first at Chittagong and then Mirpur. Five more hundreds have followed: an unbeaten 154 at Sydney, 153 at Adelaide, then 109 at Nagpur (his third consecutive hundred against Australia), 103 not out against England at Chennai, and in April 2009 he ended the series in New Zealand with 160 at Hamilton. He now leads the list of Test run-makers with 12,773 runs and 42 hundreds.

Playing hard to get

Alastair Cook

Called up as a last-minute replacement to play for England against India at Nagpur in March 2006, Cook scored a century on his Test Match debut and, at the age of 21 years and 69 days, became the youngest Englishman to reach a Test hundred in 67 years. It was such a popular achievement that an attractive young lady in the stands held up a placard reading, 'Will you marry me?'

Encouraged by this unexpected proposal, and no doubt surprised that there was more on offer for scoring Test Match centuries than just a line in *Wisden*, Cook quickly posted another six centuries, the last one against Sri Lanka at Galle on 22 December 2007. Sadly, further chance of offers of marriage were to disappear for the next fifteen months. In 27 innings he went past 50 on eleven occasions, even getting as far as 94 in one innings, but the elusive three figures refused to come.

Finally, against West Indies at Bridgetown on 26 February 2009 he reached 139 not out and the long wait was over.

A promise fulfilled

V.V.S. Laxman

After making his debut for India in 1996 the talented young Laxman seemed destined for a glittering Test career if he could overcome his early inconsistency.

The selectors still had their doubts when his 95 against Australia at Kokata in March 1998 was followed by fifteen innings that only produced 249 runs with an average of 16.67, while he was in and out of the side over the next 21 months. There was no doubt that there was a big question mark over his future.

All doubts were dismissed at Sydney in January 2000, when Laxman batted brilliantly to score 167 runs from only 198 balls against the bowling of Warne and McGrath – outshining Tendulkar, Dravid, Ganguly and the rest of the Indian side, which could only manage 94 runs between them.

With 6,741 runs from 105 Tests and an average of 45.24, Laxman has proved his right to be considered one of the best batsmen in the world today.

The cares of captaincy

Douglas Jardine

The ruthless architect of Bradman's downfall during the 1932/33 'Bodyline' series was himself a surprising victim of a crisis of confidence before the Ashes were regained.

He had enjoyed a good season in the summer preceding the tour, scoring 1,464 runs with three hundreds and an average of 52.28. This run of good form continued as soon as he arrived in Australia with 98 against a Combined Australian XI, followed by 108 not out against South Australia. Then, as pressure mounted, things started to go wrong and the next seven innings produced only 67 runs, including a 1 and 0 in the Second Test, when Australia levelled the series. As the Third Test approached Jardine took positive action: 'I insisted that the Selection Committee should consider the advisability of dropping myself. In order that they should be free to decide without embarrassment I retired from the room.' On his return he learnt that Warner, Sutcliffe, Wyatt and Hammond had found a solution that would enable Jardine to continue leading his team. They had all become aware that, in the dressing room when he was padded up and due to go in at the fall of the next wicket, Jardine would pace back and forth, ignoring everyone and muttering to himself about the state of the game. Such uncharacteristic behaviour would be overcome if he opened the batting. This compromise found favour with Gubby Allen who wrote home: 'Jardine must go in first as he is so terribly nervous he is out before he goes in.'

It did not look as if the experiment had worked when Jardine was out for three in the first innings. When England began their second innings 119 runs in front, Sutcliffe went with only seven on the board and there was a real danger that if more wickets fell quickly they would not be able to set Australia a large enough target to put the game out of their reach. It was then that Jardine rose to the challenge, conquered his nerves, and regained his batting skills. He stayed at the wicket for over four hours, while grinding out 56 runs that included only two boundaries. But England were 263 runs in front when he was finally out and thanks to runs from Hammond, Leyland and Ames, the target of 532 would prove too much for a shattered Australia, all out for 193.

A century opening partnership with Sutcliffe in the next Test and Jardine was well on the way to seeing his team taking the Ashes back to England.

Why you should always make time for an autograph

In 1996, with only one professional cricketer in their ranks, Kenya took on the mighty West Indies, double winners of the World Cup. Somewhat unsurprisingly, then, the Kenyans were all out for 166, setting the West Indies little more than three runs an over to win.

Pretty much a done deal, you'd have thought. So did Maurice Odumbe, the Kenyan captain: 'We were going out for a picnic. It was only when they started to lose wickets that we began to get serious,' he later said. Serious enough eventually to bowl the West Indies out for a paltry 93 and secure the biggest shock of the World Cup.

Man of the Match Odumbe later recalled: 'I met [Brian] Lara at a match in England several years ago before he was in the West Indies team and asked for his autograph. He said he didn't have time. When we beat them in the World Cup I went up to him and said, "A few years ago I asked for your autograph and you wouldn't give it. Now I am saying you can have mine."'

A poisoned chalice?

From what I can see, and having experienced one of the jobs myself, being England Test cricket captain is the hardest job in English sport after the England football manager. No other individual is scrutinised so relentlessly by the public, Press and the upper echelons of power of their designated sport. Once appointed – win, lose or draw – every captain enjoys a honeymoon period. But once, for whatever reason, your honeymoon period comes to an end, all the joys of the job suddenly become resoundingly clear!

Like all sportsmen, every captain wants to win, but other than that, no two are the same. Some thrive on the responsibility and it inspires them to great performances out in the middle. For others, history shows that the burden of responsibility can take its toll:

Joe Darling

Runs scored in Test Matches until appointed captain of Australia in 1899:
2,326 at 45.60

Runs scored as captain:
686 at 31.18

Ian Botham

Runs scored in Test Matches until appointed captain of England in 1980:
1,149 at 41.04

Runs scored as captain:
276 at 13.14

Jimmy Adams

Runs scored in Test Matches until appointed captain of West Indies in 1999:
2,326 at 45.60

Runs scored as captain:
686 at 31.18

Of course, history also shows those who found that captaincy – rather than being an albatross round their neck – inspired them to greater things:

Imran Khan

Runs scored in Test Matches as captain:
2,408 at 52.34

Runs scored in other Test Matches:
1,399 at 25.43

Bobby Simpson

Runs scored in Test Matches as captain:
3,623 at 54.07

Runs scored in other Test Matches:
1,246 average 33.67

Peter May

Runs scored in Test Matches as captain:
3,080 at 54.03

Runs scored in other Test Matches:
1,457 at 36.42

Graham Gooch

Runs scored in Test Matches as captain:
3,582 at 58.72

Runs scored in other Test Matches:
5,318 at 35.93

Different strokes for different folks

'I am not going to make you into a Geoffrey Boycott, but I will turn you into a better Alec Stewart than you are now.' These were the words proffered to me by Geoffrey at the outset of a coaching session he gave me in the early days of my playing career. The idea being that it is a coach's task to develop a player's existent natural talents and not make him conform to a set of skills that he might not necessarily feel comfortable with. It is an approach to coaching that I am in total agreement with. But like all the captains that I have experienced in my career, no two are the same and all placed different levels of importance on different aspects of the game.

Keith Fletcher, for example, deemed devoting time to developing cricketing skills more important than fitness. He didn't know his players very well but made a point of building a strong relationship with Mike Atherton, with a view to relaying his ideas to the team via his captain. My dad, Micky Stewart, put a great emphasis on attention to detail, planning and physical fitness when England coach. He was also the first to implement the concept of specialist coaches, introducing them for batting, bowling, wicket-keeping and fitness. David Lloyd was characteristically enthusiastic about every aspect of the game and was keen to look at introducing new ideas based on the burgeoning technology available in the game at that time, but was prevented from doing so because the costs were deemed too high.

I used to believe pretty strongly that an England coach had to be English. Nevertheless, Duncan Fletcher, and the success that he brought, proved me very wrong on that point. He managed to develop and improve the game of everyone I saw him come across as a coach and in today's game – with such a diverse set of players and skills to contend with – that is no mean feat. He is without question the best coach I ever worked with.

Along with several million other Englishmen, I used to think the same about the England football manager's job, and with the fiasco of how the FA dealt with the tenure of Sven-Goran Eriksson, felt pretty justified with my concerns. Nevertheless, the subsequent Fabio Capello regime change, and his professional take-no-prisoners approach with the England camp, seems to be now working to great effect and proving me wrong.

Nevertheless, despite my change of opinion on the managerial front – whether it be cricket or football – I still think it is very important to use home-grown players in domestic sport. It is obviously important for the future of our national sides, but is also a major benefit to the clubs as home-grown players can give you that extra few per cent because they understand the clubs and can relate to the English fans. That is one of the reasons that I was such an admirer of José Mourinho, during his reign as Chelsea manager. Other than the fact that he won us the

Premiership in consecutive seasons, he did it using more English players in key roles in his side than any other foreign coach in the League. He quickly recognised the importance of this policy, put it into practice, and enjoyed some great success as a result.

~ဆာ~

Coaches of the England Squad, 1986–2009

1986–1992
Mike Stewart

Test Match record:
Played 61, Won 12, Lost 22, Drawn 27

1992/93/94/95
Keith Fletcher

Test Match record:
Played 26, Won 5, Lost 15, Drawn 6

1995–1995/96
Ray Killingworth (also Chairman of selectors)

Test Match record:
Played 11, Won 2, Lost 3, Drawn 6

1996–1998/99
David Lloyd

Test Match record:
Played 34, Won 9, Lost 13, Drawn 34

1999
No coach (awaiting Duncan Fletcher's release for Glamorgan)

Test Match record:
Played 4, Won 1, Lost 2, Drawn 1

1999/2000–2006/07
Duncan Fletcher

Test Match record:
Played 96, Won 42, Lost 30, Drawn 24

2007–2008/09
Peter Moores

Test Match record:
Played 22, Won 8, Lost 6, Drawn 8

Test Match appearances I made under England coaches:
Mike Stewart: 22
Keith Fletcher: 23
Ray Illingworth: 8
David Lloyd: 33
Duncan Fletcher: 43

Sudden impact

In 1983, Zimbabwe played in their first World Cup. It's difficult to see how a side could make more of an impact on their debut.

Zimbabwe had never even played an official one-day international before, let alone featured in the world's greatest cricket tournament. In contrast, their Australian opponents in the first match had no fewer than 476 one-day appearances between them. The scene was set for one of the biggest shocks in the history of the World Cup. With a number of Zimbabwe wickets already down cheaply, and then Dave Houghton heading back to the pavilion with a golden duck, proceedings seemed to be going as expected. Then Duncan Fletcher came to the crease. Although another wicket fell quickly at the other end, Fletcher steadied the ship before first putting on 70 with Kevin Curran and then 75 with Iain Butchart to help his side to a respectable 239.

Having done his bit with the bat, Fletcher then went to work with the ball. He dispatched the Australian openers in quick succession before later bagging another quick brace to leave the Aussies precariously placed at 133 for 4. Before long that was 138 for 5. Despite Australia losing only another couple of wickets, and despite Rod Marsh's quick-fire unbeaten 50 from just 42 balls, the Zimbabwean bowlers restricted the favourites to 226 in their 60 overs, completing a result that only a few hours before no one would have dreamed of.

The Zimbabwean team must have celebrated fairly hard that night, as they went on to lose their other five matches in the tournament. In fact, they had to wait until their last group match of the 1992 World Cup before securing their second one-day win.

Cricket at the highest level

A group of 50 cricket lovers left Lord's on 9 April 2009 en route to the Himalayas, intending to set a new world record for the highest altitude at which a game of cricket had been played.

After carrying a full-sized artificial pitch, split into three parts, bats, stumps and pink cricket balls, which would stand out against the snow-covered mountains substituting for sight-screens, the expedition reached a frozen lake near Mount Everest three miles (17,000 feet) above sea level.

On 21 April two teams, 'Hillary' and 'Tenzing', played a match of twenty overs each side followed by tea and the raising of the Union Jack in honour of the Queen's Birthday. The match was played for charity and raised more than £250,000 for the Lord's Taverners and the Himalayan Trust.

"

It's a funny kind of month, October. For the really keen cricket fan, it's when you realise that your wife left you in May.

Dennis Norden

"

'I was Monty's double'

The 125 victims of the bowling of Monty Panesar in Test Matches would not claim to have achieved anything so prestigious as the brave impersonation by a British officer of the great English Field Marshal Montgomery to deceive the enemy during the Second World War, but among them feature some famous batsmen:

- Brendon McCullum (five times)

- AB de Villiers (four times)

- Denesh Ramdin, Andrew Symonds, Faisal Iqbal, Mohammad Yousuf (all three times each)

- Sachin Tendulkar, Rahul Dravid, Kumar Sangakkara, Inzamam-ul-Haq, Shivnarine Chanderpaul (all twice each)

- Sanath Jayasuriya, Younis Khan, Justin Langer, Adam Gilchrist, Matthew Hayden, Michael Hussey, Ramnaresh Sarwan, Mahela Jayawardene, Stephen Fleming, Hashim Amla, V.V.S. Laxman, Chris Gayle (all once each)

A knight in a gold-plated helicopter

Bouncing other men's wives up and down on his knee, he strutted around as if he owned the place. Well, he did own it. Or so we thought. Following being charged by the U.S. Securities and Exchange Commission for an alleged $8 billion investment fraud, the ECB have severed all ties with the Texan billionaire, Sir Allen Stanford, and his eponymous Twenty20 Super Series is no more. Many people will tell you that they told you so and all that, but hindsight is a wonderful thing. I'm not going to discuss the morality (or alleged lack of) of the man, but would like to take a look at some of the things that went wrong with the inaugural, and it appears now, last, Twenty20 for twenty matches between England and the Stanford Superstars.

As soon as he landed at Lord's in a gold-plated helicopter with $20 million, it was always going to be a 'show business' event, but even so, there were a number of aspects that should never have been allowed to unfold. For a start we shouldn't have played under the name of England because when you represent your country it's because you are playing against another country. They could have been called 'Kevin Pietersen's Heroes' – just anything but England. Not that that contributed to why they lost.

The Stanford Superstars had a six-week training camp to focus and prepare for the event and as a result, played exceptionally good cricket and deserved to win. Their nerves were clearly jangling a little early on with a few misfields but they soon got over that and played very well. Although the floodlights weren't brilliant, they also caught well. After a long season, England had taken a well-earned break but consequently went out to the Caribbean just before the tournament. Now they had known about England's involvement and the money on offer for four months prior to the event so there were issues that they should have resolved long before they got out there.

Alastair Cook hit the nail on the head when he said that they were playing for the money. Although the ECB were quick to shout him down and point out that they had signed the deal with Stanford in order to further grass-roots cricket here and in the Caribbean, they should have given it all some more thought. Although the majority of players would obviously approve of a financial boost to help develop the game at grass-roots level, as far as they were concerned – as professional sportsmen – they were going out there to win the prize money on offer to them. Whether you are playing for 50 pence, a fiver or a million dollars a man, everything needs to be considered in order to give yourself the best chance of winning. The management should have recognised that and dealt with it accordingly.

For example, something as seemingly simple as how they were going to divvy up the money. Initially it was only the eleven who were going to get the million dollars, and the four squad players that missed out were going to share a million dollars. So when KP had to go up to James Anderson, put his arm round his shoulders to say 'sorry mate you're not playing tomorrow', that was $750,000 which Anderson was missing out on. They eventually decided on the morning of the game that they were going to share the money equally between the whole squad, but issues like that should have been sorted earlier so that the players could focus on the cricket itself.

The Press also played their part. There was a lot of negativity about the event itself and whether the players – in the current economic climate – should be able to win such substantial sums of money to win a single game of cricket. Well, no one seems to mind when Roger Federer or Tiger Woods wins a million or is paid a similar sum just to turn up for an exhibition match, so why should cricket be any different? As professional sportsmen, they can only turn up and play for what's on offer. Nevertheless, whether right or wrong, there is no question that it was another distraction that ensured that, by the time they took to the field, they looked like rabbits in the headlights – or sub-standard floodlights anyway. Not that that can be used as an excuse because – as we all know – it's the same for both sides.

As far as the Superstars were concerned, having bowled England out for 99, Chris Gayle went out and had the time of his life, hitting five fours and five sixes to an unbeaten 65 off 45 balls. At the other end was this guy Andre Fletcher, who most of us had never heard of. Following them effortlessly breezing over the line without a wicket down, Nasser Hussain asked the Man of the Match Darren Sammy how he was going to spend all his winnings. Anticipating the inevitable list of flash cars and other luxury items he was a little taken aback when Sammy – following thanking God and his team-mates – explained that he would invest it sensibly in property in the measured response akin to an accountant. It was obvious: to most of the players in the Superstars it was a life-changing win. They wanted it more, and that's why they won.

As far as the England side were concerned, as we all know, they came home with nothing and so – in light of how seriously the West Indian players took it – it would have been interesting to see how differently the England players would have approached it this year and the following years after that. Unfortunately, we'll never know.

Twenty20 – Facts and figures

England's defeat in Antigua against the Stanford Superstars last November was not the worst on record, as England supporters may have assumed.

The top three biggest defeats on record are:

- Australia (102-0) needed only 10.2 overs to beat Sri Lanka (101) at Cape Town in 2007

- South Africa (132-0) needed only 11.3 overs to beat Pakistan (129) at Johannesburg in 2007

- Stanford Superstars (101-0) needed 13.1 overs to beat England (99) at Antigua in 2008

There have, in fact, been 11 innings totals lower than England's 99

- *Lowest innings total:* Kenya's 67 from 17.2 overs v. Ireland, Belfast, 2008

- *Highest innings total:* Sri Lanka's 260 for six v. Kenya, Johannesburg, 2007

- *Most sixes in a match:* 24, New Zealand v. India, Christchurch, 2009

Cricket One Hundred Years Ago

1909 Ashes series in England:
Australia 2 England 1 Drawn 2

County Championship:
1 Kent, 2 Lancashire, 3 Yorkshire

Record most runs in a day by one side:
645 5 Surrey v Hampshire, The Oval, 6 May 1909 – J. Hobbs
and E. Hayes in second-wicket partnership of 371 runs in
165 minutes (remains the fourth-highest of all time)

Record tenth wicket partnership:
235 in 140 minutes – F. Woolley and A. Fielder for Kent v.
Worcestershire at Stourbridge, 6 and 7 July 1909
(remains the fourth-highest of all time)

Foundation of ICC (Imperial Cricket Conference)

George Headley, born 30 May 1909
22 Tests for West Indies 1929–1953
2,190 runs, 10 hundreds, 60.83 average, 14 catches
103 First Class: 9,921 runs, 33 hundreds, 69.86 average,
76 catches
Wisden Cricketer of the Year 1934

Bill Voce, born 8 August 1909
27 Tests for England
308 runs, 13.39 average, 15 catches

98 wickets, 27.88 average
426 First Class: 525 runs, 4 hundreds, 19.21 average, 288
catches
1,558 wickets, 23.08 average
Wisden Cricketer of the Year 1933

Ↄ₯₯

My Test Match Century

– Introduction –

Achievements in the Test Match arena continue to be the true measure of ability for players and all lovers of the game of cricket. Every innings played by every batsman is important, whether its contribution to the team's final total is large or small. But some innings in first-class cricket – especially Test Matches – can have a dramatic impact, depending on the context in which the innings was played and its influence on the result of the match. A batsman scoring a handful of runs to save his team from following-on, or a tail-ender seeing out the final overs of a match to stave off defeat, can be as big a hero as any batsman who scores a century or more. Naturally, it is the century-makers we remember the most, their frequency recorded and tabulated within the pages of the record books. But some of those centuries had far less influence over the final structure of the matches in which they were made than smaller and shorter innings at other times. So it is not always the highest score that impresses the most. It could be the batsman who hits the final few runs required for victory against all the odds that catches the eye. And it is sometimes how an innings ends rather than its content that makes it memorable.

I have asked Brian Rendell, historian and statistician, to examine every individual batsman's Test Match scores from 1 to 100 (and there have been over 50,000 of them), to identify those which stand out from the rest. Each choice, in ascending order from the solitary single up to the coveted three-figures, has been influenced by a variety of circumstances. Our final selections are, I believe, the 100 most unique innings in the history of Test Match cricket and I am proud to have been playing in several of the matches in which some of these innings have taken place.

Of course, as a new Test Match will be in progress somewhere in the world almost every day of the year, any one of the selections could be replaced by a new, more important, dramatic or historic innings at that score. That is the magic of Test Match cricket and I hope readers will have fun examining scorecards and reports much more closely in future while searching for additions or replacements to the list that has been compiled for this book.

1

First out

Nathaniel Thompson b Hill 1
Australia v. England. Melbourne, 15 March 1877

The fourth group of English cricketers to tour Australia were all professionals under the captaincy of James Lillywhite. They arrived at the beginning of November 1876 and their lack of batting strength was exploited at every opportunity as they struggled against the various State and country teams put up against them. There was a growing awareness of the improved standards of Australian cricket and a belief that it was now equal to anything that the England players could offer. It was time to 'test' the truth of that belief with a selection of the best eleven Australian cricketers from the States of Victoria and New South Wales.

The actual choice of players for this 'Test Match' – the first time such a game had ever been played – created heated interstate arguments, but as the game was to be played in Melbourne the Victorians dominated the selection process. Nevertheless, it was a player from New South Wales, the great Fred Spofforth, who was one of the first names put forward. But as he wanted his team-mate Billy Murdoch as wicket-keeper and the Victorians were determined to have their own man John Blackham, Spofforth declined his invitation. There were others who preferred not to be involved but eventually a strong side was put together, although, because of the absentees, it was generally considered to be inferior to the England team. Soon the disputes were forgotten and all Australian cricket stood behind their team in what was agreed would be the most important match ever to be played in the colonies.

The game began with Charles Bannerman and Nat Thompson opening the Australian innings. Thompson was a right-hand bat and useful medium-pace bowler who had been playing first-class cricket for twenty years. Both openers scored a single apiece before Thompson was bowled by Allen Hill in the fourth over, from only the sixth ball he faced, to earn the dubious distinction of being the first batsman in history to be dismissed in a Test Match. His opening partner went on to score the first Test century (165) but Australia could not capitalise on their first-innings lead and collapsed in their second innings for only 104 with Nat Thompson making only a slight improvement on his first attempt by scoring seven. However, to the delight of their supporters, the Australians upset all the odds and won the first 'Test Match' by 45 runs.

Two weeks later the English tourists returned to Melbourne, seeking a chance to get their revenge against another representative side. This time the arguments about selection were less heated and Spofforth came into the side as well as his favourite wicket-keeper Murdoch. But the colonials were less successful against a more determined England team, which won by four wickets. Nat Thompson had kept his place as opener and made an improved contribution of eighteen and 41. He continued to play first-class cricket for another three years but was unable to accept David Gregory's invitation to tour England in 1878 and never appeared in another Test Match.

2

Last ball winner

Stephen Boock not out 2
New Zealand v. West Indies. Dunedin, 13 February 1980

The West Indies had come to New Zealand with the reputation for being the best side in the world after beating Australia 2-0 in Australia. New Zealand, on the other hand, not having won a match for two years, were hoping to crown their celebrations of 50 years of Test cricket by fighting tooth and nail for victory.

In the First Test, the West Indian batsmen found it difficult to adjust to new conditions and the whole team was unsettled by some dubious umpiring decisions, so that, in a low-scoring match, New Zealand eventually only needed 104 runs to win. Magnificent bowling by Holding, Garner and Croft reduced New Zealand to 54-7 before some fine aggressive batting from Hadlee and Cairns brought them back into the game. Hadlee went at 73-8 and Cairns at 100-9 to bring Boock to the wicket still needing four runs to win. Somehow Boock managed to survive the last five balls from Holding's over and Garner started the last over of the day to Troup who had played a valiant supporting role while Cairns had brought them close to victory. The two batsmen took a bye off the first ball, although Boock, hoping to keep his well-set partner on strike, was almost run out when sent back by Troup after calling for a second. Boock survived an lbw appeal off the second ball and then kept the next two balls out of his stumps, but New Zealand were still three runs short with the last two balls to come. With West Indian fielders crowding around him, Boock squeezed two runs backward of point to level the scores. He missed the last ball of the match but it hit his pads and went away to backward square-leg while both batsmen crossed and made their ground for the winning run.

3

Handled the Ball

William Russell Endean handled the ball 3
South Africa v. England. Cape Town, 5 January 1957

Nicknamed 'Endless' Endean by the Australians when stubbornly occupying the crease for hours during the South African tour in 1953, he was the backbone of his country's batting for 28 Tests during the 1950s.

After losing the First Test, South Africa went into the Second Test of the 1956/57 series desperate not to go 2-0 down. Much depended on Endean when South Africa were finally set 385 to win and they reached 41-2 at close of play on the fourth day, with Endean three not out. The following morning he set himself up for another lengthy occupation of the crease and survived for 40 minutes without adding to his score. Then he padded away a ball from Laker that pitched innocuously outside the off-stump only to see the ball spin up into the air and start falling back onto his stumps. Endean instinctively diverted the ball with his hand and fell foul of Law 33 of the 1947 Code of The Laws of Cricket – Out Handled the Ball, which reads 'either batsman on appeal shall be out Handled the Ball if he wilfully touches the ball while in play with the hand not holding the bat unless he does so with the consent of the opposite side'.

So Endean earned the dubious distinction of becoming the first batsman to suffer a 'Handled the Ball' dismissal in Test cricket and a shocked South Africa slumped to 72 all out to lose by 312 runs.

4

An opportunity missed to fill his boots

Brian Lara c Boucher b Zondeki 4
West Indies v. South Africa. St John's, Antigua, 1 May 2005

When Brian Lara went to the wicket with West Indies 345-2 in reply to South Africa's 588-6 declared, six hundreds had already been scored during the first three days of the match. *Wisden* would write later that when Lara strode out, 'Nothing seemed more certain than another huge innings' – a reasonable expectation from the batsman who almost twelve months earlier had broken the record for the highest individual Test innings with 400 not out on the same ground. Who would have imagined that Lara's personal contribution to a West Indies final total of 747 would be one boundary from 29 balls?

Gayle went on to reach 317 followed by Chanderpaul and Bravo recording hundreds of their own, creating a new record of eight hundreds in one Test that has yet to be equalled. There was only time for South Africa to score 127 1 from 31 overs in their second innings and the match ended in a draw with no opportunity for Lara to make amends for failing to help himself to a larger share of the feast of runs on offer.

5

Forgetting his lines

Glenn McGrath not out 5
Australia v. England. Old Trafford, 15 August 2005

The summer of 2005 in England was the scene of one of the most thrilling Ashes Series in the History of Test Match cricket. The Australians, still regarded as possessing the best team in the world, came to face a revived England squad that had just enjoyed a record-breaking year with seven wins out of seven, including 4-0 against the West

Indies the previous summer, followed by their first Series victory in South Africa for over 40 years. There were high expectations that, after losing eight consecutive Ashes Series over a new record period of eighteen years, at long last England stood a genuine chance of recovering the famous urn. Those hopes were dashed by Australia's victory in the opening Test at Lord's, but ran high again when England came back to win the Second Test convincingly.

Much depended on the Third Test at Old Trafford: victory for either side could seal the series. Once again England proved to be the stronger and in their second innings Australia were set 423 to win, or at least 100 overs to play out a draw. Australia could only reach 264-7 with 31 overs left to play and the match seemed to have turned in favour of England. Then Warne joined Ponting who was playing a great captain's innings to stave off defeat, which might even have put them in range of an incredible victory. They added another 76 before Warne fell caught behind off Flintoff, and soon after at 6.28pm a ball from Steve Harmison found Ponting's glove to bring in the last man, McGrath, at 345-9 with four overs left for play.

It seemed nothing could prevent an England victory but Brett Lee and McGrath bravely poked and jabbed their way through to the final over. With McGrath on strike Australian supporters took heart when they remembered that, despite being the worst batsman in the team by far, Glenn McGrath had managed to defy the England bowlers in his three previous innings and had yet to be dismissed in the series. Could 'Pigeon', so-called by his team-mates because of his spindly legs, make it four? The Australian dressing room sent a message out instructing him to receive the ball standing forward of his crease so that he could not be out leg-before. Unfortunately, he forgot that to avoid being run-out he would have to quickly make his ground after connecting with the ball or seeing it go past him to the wicket-keeper standing well back to Harmison. England wanted to keep him on strike so they positioned Hoggard at short-leg with instructions to rush to the stumps immediately the ball was hit or missed and so prevent a quick single. All went according to plan off the first ball and no run was possible, but back in the pavilion the Australians screamed in despair when they realised that McGrath had stayed out of his crease. But anxious to have another chance of bowling McGrath out, Hoggard had quickly thrown the ball back to the bowler and had not noticed the opportunity for a run-out to win the match. Before McGrath could forget his instructions a second time, and the England fielders realise his strategy, he scrambled a single off the next ball and Brett Lee batted out the over to earn Australia a draw.

6

Bookies' favourite

Darren Gough not out 6
England v. South Africa. Centurion, 18 January 2000

With South Africa 2-0 up, England's hopes of salvaging some pride from the series with a win in the fifth and final Test at Centurion, after reducing the home side to 155-6 on the first day, seemed doomed to disappointment when bad weather prevented any play on the second, third or fourth days. But the South African captain Hansie Cronje had other ideas and half-an-hour before play started on the last day he approached the England captain Nasser Hussain with an unexpected suggestion that they might try to make a game of it. If South Africa could add another 100 runs to their score off 30 overs and then England forfeited their first innings and South Africa their second, there could be a target of 255 runs from 73 overs for England to chase at a reasonable 3.5 runs per over. A cautious Hussein declined, uncertain about the condition of the wicket after three days sweating under covers. England might be skittled out for a handful of runs on an unplayable wicket and then there would have been a lot of questions to answer.

Play began on time and after having a good look for ten overs at how the wicket played under bright sunny skies, Hussain left the field and asked Cronje if the offer was still open. Delighted at the change of mind, Cronje let South Africa bat on for another seventeen overs before declaring at 248-8, leaving England 76 overs to reach 249 at the even easier rate of 3.27 runs per over. In fact, no provision existed under the Laws for a team to forfeit its first innings, although it was expected to be introduced later that year, and the scorers were instructed to record England's first innings as 0-0 declared as if their opening batsmen had taken the field and received a ball or two. Cronje promptly forfeited the South African second innings, as the Laws allowed, and England began batting with confidence that victory was within their grasp, eventually reaching 228 for the loss of five wickets.

Then two more wickets fell for eight runs and Gough came in with thirteen runs still needed. All hopes rested on Vaughan who was still there after sharing an earlier century partnership with Stewart, but he was bowled by Hayward almost immediately and Silverwood now joined Gough with nine runs still needed from the final thirteen balls. Silverwood took a single, then scrambled a two followed by a lucky boundary that should have been stopped by a fielder blinded by the sun. Encouraged by his partner's good fortune, Gough pulled the first ball of the last over of the match to the boundary and England had won to the joy of many hundreds of travelling England supporters who, when the day started had never expected to witness such a result.

At the time this was seen as a memorable and entertaining climax to a match heading to a dull and disappointing draw if the Laws had been strictly followed by captains not prepared to risk defeat in order that either side could win. Unfortunately, five months later, it was revealed that Cronje had accepted a bribe from a bookmaker to initiate a positive result and although he insisted his motives were 'for the good of the game', the fact that financial reward formed part of his motivation tainted the match forever.

7

The best laid plans

Bill Johnston not out 7
Australia v. West Indies. Melbourne, 3 January 1952

Desperately trying to level the series, West Indies were confident they could dismiss Australia for less than 260 on the last day of the Fourth Test. Everything went according to plan and when last man Johnston joined Ring, Australia were still 38 runs short after 'those little friends of mine Ramadhin and Valentine' had taken eight wickets between them. To everyone's surprise the runs kept coming and when the final eight-ball over arrived Australia needed only three runs to win. First Johnston and then Ring took a single apiece and the scores were level. Johnston turned the penultimate ball of the match to leg and what might have been the first tied Test in history ended in Australia's favour.

8

He'll never succeed in England!

Don Bradman b Tate 8
Australia v. England. Trent Bridge, 14 June 1930

Bradman made his Test debut against England in the 1928/29 series in Australia, and after a false start in the First Test, with scores of eighteen and one, he was dropped for the Second but returned for the last three to score 449 runs, including two centuries, at an average of 89.8. But some critics, including England Test veteran Percy Fender, covering the series for the *London Star* and *Daily News*, found fault with his technique. They asserted that his grip on the bat handle was wrong, leading to uncontrolled miss-hits and that only good luck had sent catches out of reach of fieldsmen. Most dismissed his chances of scoring many runs in England and Fender declared that he was 'one of the most curious mixtures of good and bad batting I had ever seen'.

In the Australian domestic season the following winter Bradman scored 1,586 runs at an average of 113.28 and his selection for the tour of England was automatic. Seeming to have proved his English detractors wrong, Bradman became the first touring batsman to score 1,000 runs in England before June, including two double centuries, and created enormous public interest. He went into the First Test at Trent Bridge with 1,230 runs from fourteen innings and it appeared that Fender and Co. were about to be shown the error of their misjudgements.

Play was delayed on the second day after heavy rain had fallen on the uncovered pitch overnight and Australia did not start their first innings until midafternoon when England were all out for 270. Maurice Tate immediately took advantage of the conditions and claimed the wickets of Ponsford, Woodfull and Bradman, while Australia only had sixteen runs on the board. Being bowled by Tate for a score of eight refuelled all the doubts about Bradman's ability at Test Match level and he was under enormous pressure when he returned to the wicket in the second innings after Australia's first wicket had fallen for only twelve runs. Conclusively proving his critics wrong, Bradman made 131, although Australia finished well short of the 429 runs needed to win. Bradman went on to accumulate a record total of 974 runs for the series at an average of 139.4, including two double centuries and a treble century at Leeds.

But for 48 hours that first innings score of eight must have preyed on Bradman's mind and provided the motivation finally to force his detractors to eat their words.

9

You've been Mankaded!

Ian Redpath Run out 9
Australia v. West Indies. Adelaide, 29 January 1969

During India's match against an Australian XI at Sydney in 1947, the slow left-hand bowler Vinoo Mankad was in the act of delivering a ball, when he noticed that Bill Brown, the Australian opener, was more than a yard out of his ground while backing-up from the non-receiver's end. Mankad stopped and beckoned Brown back behind the popping-crease with a crooked finger. This warning was hailed as one of the most sporting gestures ever seen on the ground, but went unheeded by Brown, who committed the same error later in the innings, giving Mankad no option but to stop and turn to break the wicket and run Brown out.

Four weeks later, during the Second Test at Sydney, Mankad again noticed that, as he entered his delivery stride to bowl, Brown was backing-up well out of his crease. Without a warning Mankad stopped and whipped the bails off to run Brown out for a second time. This method of dismissal immediately became known as a 'Mankad' and if a batsman was given out this way he was said to have been 'Mankaded'.

It would be another 22 years before it was repeated in a Test Match and again it was an Australian batsman. On the last day of the Fourth Test at Adelaide, with West Indies pressing to level the series 2-2, Ian Redpath came in at 185-2 with Australia looking to score 360 and go 3-1 up and win the series. With the stakes so high Charlie Griffith, the West Indian fast bowler, could not resist the opportunity to stop in mid-delivery, having seen Redpath backing-up well down the pitch, and run him out when he had only scored nine. Redpath accepted his fate with good grace, saying afterwards – 'like an idiot I decided to go walkabout'. His captain's thoughts may have been less charitable, as it was only thanks to a desperate last-wicket stand, lasting 26 balls, that Australia survived with a draw.

Between 1969 and 1979 there were two other instances of 'Mankading' in Test cricket but the Laws have now been changed so that a bowler may no longer 'Mankad' a batsman once he has actually entered his delivery stride, although a bowler can run out a non-striker who has strayed outside his crease after the bowler has started his run-up, as long as it is before he has entered the stride in which the delivery swing is made.

10

So long for so little

Godfrey Evans not out 10
England v. Australia. Adelaide, 5 and 6 January 1947

When England travelled on their first post-war tour of Australia in 1946/47 the team desperately lacked genuine speed from its fast bowlers, whereas Australia now had a number of young men, Lindwall and Miller to the fore, posing a real threat to England batsmen who had not faced such furious pace for seven years. By the Fourth Test Australia were 2-0 up, both by innings victories, and England were struggling to stay competitive. Thanks to Compton, Hutton, Washbrook and Hardstaff, England's first innings of 460 gave Australia their first real challenge and a good second innings might just have given England's bowlers a platform from which to strike back and perhaps seize an unexpected victory.

When the eighth wicket fell at 255 giving England a flimsy lead of 228 it looked much more like another win for Australia. Evans joined Compton at the wicket with 45 minutes left for play. Up to then there had been no indication that Evans was anything other than an exceptional wicket-keeper, who did not bat at the bottom of the order because there were always the even lesser batting talents of Bedser, Wright or Voce available to occupy those positions. Five innings in that Series so far of 5, 9, 17, 0* and 0 inspired little confidence that he would be at the wicket for long. Getting his head down, Evans survived until stumps, although without scoring, and then he astonished everyone the next day by staying with Compton long enough to see him reach his second century of the match during a partnership of 85 runs. Only ten of those runs came from the bat of Evans, and he had established a world record by taking 95 minutes to score even his first run, and remained not out after two and a half hours, giving Hammond the opportunity to declare 313 runs ahead without risking defeat but with an opportunity to bowl Australia out.

Victory in those circumstances would have been the icing on the cake but avoiding defeat was a victory in itself and England could look ahead with more confidence than at any other time during the previous two months of the Series. In recognition of his valiant, back-to-the-wall performance, Winston Churchill sent Evans a telegram message – 'Never did one man bat for so long for so little.' And in seasons to come Evans would go on to establish himself as a more than useful middle-order batsman.

11

Double figures

Bert Sutcliffe b Wardle 11
New Zealand v. England. Auckland, 28 March 1955

New Zealand played their first Test Match in 1929 and 26 years later made their twenty-first attempt to achieve victory over a confident England who had already beaten them by eight wickets just eight days earlier after coming on from a 3-1 series win in Australia.

The presence of Bert Sutcliffe, generally recognised as standing side-by-side with Neil Harvey as the best two left-handers of their generation, gave New Zealand supporters some cause for hope but the rest of the batting line-up was extremely frail. Their worst fears were eventually realised when New Zealand crashed to the lowest score in Test Match History with a second innings total of just 26 runs. Sutcliffe was the only batsman to reach double figures with the other ten making just fifteen runs between them.

One can only imagine what Sutcliffe might have achieved if he had played in a stronger side, but even so, his eighteen-year career record was outstanding with 2,727 runs from 42 Tests at an average of 40.16 runs, despite never appearing on the winning side.

12

All in a day

Ridley Jacobs c Atherton b Caddick 12
West Indies v. England. Lord's, 30 June 2000

Wisden reported that after a first innings total of 134 in response to West Indies 267, England's captain called the players together in the dressing room and 'read his team the riot act' before leading them onto the field. The England bowlers responded and when Ridley Jacobs went to the wicket the West Indies had collapsed to 24-5. He was not there for long but was the only player to reach double figures with twelve runs out of 54.

It was the only day in Test history that contained a part of all four innings with a total of 21 wickets falling.

13

Unlucky for some

Mike Atherton b Warne 13
England v. Australia. The Oval, 23 August 2001

In reply to Australia's massive 641-4 declared, Mike Atherton was the first batsman out when England began their reply, after scoring thirteen. It was his last Test before retirement and the seventh time he had been dismissed after reaching that ominous number for those of a superstitious nature. No other batsman has lost his wicket after scoring thirteen in Test Matches as often as Atherton, a record he would probably prefer to forget.

14

Youngest ever debut

Mushtaq Mohammad lbw Hall 14
Pakistan v. West Indies. Lahore, 29 March 1959

Mushtaq Mohammad made his Test debut as the youngest player ever to play in a Test Match when apparently aged only fifteen years 124 days. The recording of births in Pakistan after Partition were unreliable and an even younger age of fourteen years 227 days has been claimed for Hasan Raja when making his Test debut for Pakistan against Zimbabwe in 1996, although that has been rejected by the Pakistan Cricket Board. So Mushtaq Mohammad keeps the record. Going in at 180-6 he was out lbw for fourteen to Wes Hall as the first victim of the first-ever hat-trick taken by a West Indian bowler.

Mushtaq Mohammad went on to play in 48 more Tests over the next eighteen years, scoring ten centuries and ended with a Test career average of 40.53.

15

'Overshadowed by Grace'

Joey Palmer c Barlow b Briggs 15
Australia v. England. Kennington Oval, 13 August 1886

The fifth Australian team to tour England was not as strong as it could have been, lacking several leading players, a strong captain, and losing the services of star fast bowler Spofforth to an injury early in the tour.

Joey Palmer had begun his career as an outstanding medium pace spin bowler in the early 1880s, but as his powers faded he devoted time to improving his batting, moving steadily up the batting order from tail-ender to opener. There was little he could do about Australia's collapse in the first innings of the Third Test, other than being top scorer with fifteen out of 68 after W.G. Grace had made his highest Test score of 170 in England's 434. Palmer was held back in the second innings but going in at 30-4 chasing 336 to avoid an innings defeat his 35 made little difference. This would be his last Test appearance as he fractured a kneecap soon after returning to Australia, which prevented him playing again at the highest level.

16

Hindu hero

Anil Dalpat not out 16
Pakistan v. England. Karachi, 6 March 1984

The first Hindu to represent Pakistan at cricket, Anil's debut was a spectacular success. He came in to bat in the second innings at 38-5 with Pakistan still needing a further 28 runs to win. Holding his nerve while two more wickets went down, he steered them to safety at 66-7 with top score of the innings and Pakistan went one-up in the series.

17

Timed out in 'timeless' Test

Les Ames not out 17
England v. South Africa. Durban, 14 March 1939

Slow batting on docile pitches and an overcautious approach on Hammond's part as England's captain produced only one result from the first four Tests of England's winter tour of South Africa in 1938/39. But the Rules for the tour stated that with England only one Test up, the final Test should be played to a finish. As England did not have to sail home more than a week later it was assumed that there would be plenty of time to finish the match.

In their first innings South Africa used up nearly all the first three days and by the end of the fifth day had only just started their second. At the end of the seventh day England needed 443 runs to win with nine wickets in hand leaving three playing days before the England party would have to leave to catch their ship at Cape Town. But not for the first time, the weather intervened and torrential rain cancelled out a complete day's play. Even so, England's batsmen stuck to their task and a double century from Edrich, plus supporting centuries from Gibbs and Hammond, took them to 611-4 when Ames came in to bat still needing 85 runs to win. On the brink of a sensational victory, even after losing another wicket, but now only 42 runs away from victory with five wickets in hand, the rains came again and the tenth day of play ended at 5.45pm with a result still awaited. But there seemed little doubt that Ames, who had top-scored with 84 in England's first innings, would see them home to victory if play could be resumed the following morning. But time had finally run out and if England were to catch their ship, which sailed on 17 March, the next three days had to be taken up with the train journey from Durban to Cape Town, or else be stranded in South Africa for another two weeks.

So the 'timeless' Test as it would become known, ended in the draw no one had expected and after nine days' play, two Sunday rest days and one day's play lost to the weather, Ames will be eternally poised at seventeen not out – unless the 22 players can gather together again at some ground in cricket's Valhalla and reach the result that eluded their titanic efforts while on terra firma below.

18

The better half

Victor Trumper b Hirst 18
Australia v. England. Edgbaston, 30 May 1902

The highlight of the Australian tour of 1902 was the batting of Victor Trumper. His ability to dominate any bowling on any wicket, wet or dry, was outstanding. And during a very wet summer indeed, he rarely opened an Australian innings on a perfect batting strip. His batting became one of the talking points of the cricketing world and he outshone the rest of the Australian batting line-up, which included such luminaries as Noble, Hill, Armstrong, Duff and Darling.

Birmingham was to host its first ever Test Match, also the first of the series, during the last three days of May and it followed on immediately from the drawn match against MCC at Lord's where Trumper had made a century in the first innings followed by 86 in the second. The Australians were undefeated at this stage of the tour after four wins and three draws, but were now about to face perhaps the strongest batting side ever to represent England in which all eleven had scored centuries in first-class cricket.

Rain interrupted England's first innings and if there was going to be any chance of a result many thought that MacLaren should have closed the innings earlier on the second day. But he had timed his declaration perfectly and put the Australians in on a drying pitch. They were all back in the pavilion after 85 minutes making their lowest-ever Test score of a mere 36 runs, half of them coming from the bat of Trumper. England looked forward to finishing the game off on the final day but rain delayed the start until 5.15 in the afternoon and the chance was lost. The Australians put the memory of this match behind them and went on to win one of the closest contested Series 2-1, during which Trumper made a century before lunch at Old Trafford.

19

One-armed hero

Colin Cowdrey not out 19
England v. West Indies. Lord's, 25 June 1963

Needing only 234 to win, Cowdrey came in at 31-3 to face a rampant Wes Hall pitching the ball consistently short from the Pavilion End where there was no sight-screen. Cowdrey had his left arm broken when trying to fend off a ball from hitting him in the face and retired hurt at nineteen not out.

Close and Barrington gave a typically gutsy response to the situation but when Close was eventually out at 219-8 England still needed fifteen runs to win with the last pair at the wicket as Cowdrey was not expected to bat. Over the next five overs Allen and Shackleton managed to score seven singles and when the last over arrived eight runs were required by a desperate England already one down in the series. Hall was still bowling, as he had done continuously since play started at 2.40 that afternoon after a delay for bad weather. Shackleton swung and missed the first ball but then tapped away a quick single and this was followed by a second when Allen turned the third ball down to long leg. Shackleton missed the fourth ball and was slow to respond to Allen's call to sneak a bye, being run out by West Indian skipper Worrell beating him in a race to the stumps at the bowler's end.

The match looked all over with victory to the West Indies but to everyone's amazement Cowdrey emerged from the pavilion with his left arm in plaster from wrist to elbow. Fortunately, he did not have to take strike as Allen and Shackleton had crossed when making their unsuccessful attempt to run a bye. Speaking later, Cowdrey explained that if he had to face Hall he had intended to turn around to bat left-handed to protect his broken arm. Allen defended the fifth ball successfully and when Hall ran in to bowl the last ball of the match there were still four possible results. Allen resisted the temptation to go for glory and risk dismissal and the game ended in a draw.

Cowdrey did not play again that season but was eventually able to join the England team halfway through a winter tour of India and resumed his Test career immediately with a century.

20

The Little Master

Hanif Mohammad b Tattersall 20
Pakistan v. England. Lord's, 14 June 1954

Pakistan had only played five Tests since their debut against India in 1952 when they arrived in England in the summer of 1954. Their first Test at Lord's was a huge disappointment for them when play could not begin until the afternoon of the fourth day. By close of play they had crawled to 50-3 with opener Hanif Mohammad still there at eleven not out after batting for two and a quarter hours. The next morning Pakistan collapsed to 87 all out with Hanif making top score with twenty. England did little better and Pakistan began their second innings only 30 runs behind. Determined not to lose their first ever Test on English soil, Pakistan dourly settled in to bat out a draw on the final afternoon, reaching 121-3 with a contribution of 39 from Hanif, who had shown monumental patience in both innings to score a total of 59 runs in five and a half hours.

The best of four brothers who played for Pakistan, Hanif became known as 'The Little Master' and scored centuries against every Test-playing country except South Africa.

21

Middle-order mainstay

Barry Sinclair c Salahuddin b Pervez 21
New Zealand v. Pakistan. Rawalpindi, 30 March 1965

Barry Sinclair established himself as the backbone of the New Zealand middle-order but in 21 Tests was never on the winning side.

New Zealand began their second innings at Rawalpindi 143 runs behind Pakistan and after a resolute second wicket stand of 39 between Sinclair and Jarvis, lost their last eight wickets for 37 runs crashing to 79 all out. Not even Sinclair could prevent the collapse with top score of 21, although it took Pakistan nearly three hours to get them out.

22

The Ashes crown the year

Denis Compton not out 22
England v. Australia. Kennington Oval, 19 August 1953

After almost nineteen years England finally regained the Ashes just before 3pm on the fourth day of the final Test of the series. Needing 132 to win and with a large and nervous crowd remaining subdued by disbelief that it was actually happening, perhaps with the memory of being skittled out for 52 at the same ground five years earlier still fresh in their minds, England crawled their way to the winning total, taking over two and a half hours to score the last 94 runs.

It seemed entirely appropriate that Edrich and Compton should be at the wicket when the winning shot was made. Those two, plus England's captain Hutton, were all that remained from the England team that had represented England before the Second World War and they had suffered disappointment together in all the four previous Ashes series since 1938.

The crowd, now delirious with joy, swarmed onto the field to cheer Hutton and his team on the pavilion balcony. Denis Compton, the darling of English cricket in the early post-war years, had appropriately made the winning hit that restored England's pride in the same year that saw the Coronation of Queen Elizabeth ll. Of the 1,501 runs he had scored against Australia those 22 would surely be the most treasured of all.

23

So little for so long

Martin Snedden b Alderman 23
New Zealand v. Australia. Wellington, 16 and 17 March 1990

There was only enough time to fit in a single Test against Australia after a triangular one-day tournament and most of the play in the first two days was restricted by bad weather. As a consequence the pitch was ideal for seam bowling and runs were hard to come by. Near the end of the second day tail-ender Martin Snedden was sent in as nightwatchman at 89-2 and he remained not out at close of play without scoring. The next morning he scored six runs then set a Test record by not scoring again for 94 minutes while New Zealand laboriously overhauled the Australian first innings total of 110. Snedden was finally out for 23 after staying at the wicket for three hours in all, and eventually New Zealand cruised to a nine-wicket victory.

24

Out twice the same day

W.G. Grace c Bannerman b Ferris 24
England v. Australia. Lord's, 17 July 1888

Anyone seeing the great 'Champion' W.G. Grace bat once a day would count themselves fortunate – to see him walking to the middle to start a new innings twice in the same day would be an unexpected bonus. That is, unless you were an England supporter and had just seen England collapse earlier that day to 53 all out and were now seeing them return with a target of 124 to win on an almost unplayable wicket. England had started the second day at 18-3 in reply to Australia's 116, but within an hour Grace was out, plus six others, while adding a mere 35 runs. Australia themselves collapsed to 18-7 but finally managed to reach 60 to set England the impossible task of making the highest innings total of the match. Casting all caution aside, Grace began batting as if there was nothing to fear and raced to 24 out of the first 34 on the board before being caught by Bannerman off Ferris and English hopes of victory went with him. His 24 was the highest individual score of the match and he was the only English batsman to reach double figures in both innings.

25

Starts a riot

Basil Butcher c Parks b D'Oliveira 25
West Indies v. England. Jamaica, 10 February 1968

Until a riot broke out in the stands on the afternoon of the fourth day, England appeared to be winning the match comfortably. The West Indies' reply to England's first innings total of 376 was a mere 143 and they followed on 233 behind. Half the side were out for 204 before Sobers and Butcher began to turn things round with a century partnership. But when Butcher was adjudged to have been caught low down by wicket-keeper Parks diving on the leg-side the crowd were upset by the decision given by Umpire Sang Hue and responded with a hail of bottles thrown on to the ground. The players were forced to retreat to the pavilion for safety while Police took over an hour to restore order.

Despite being shaken by the incident and apprehensive of a repeat outbreak of crowd violence Sobers batted magnificently for a century when play resumed, ably supported by batsmen from the lower order. England needed only 158 to win but almost lost the match on a fiery pitch collapsing to 68-8 before the game ended as a draw.

26

First to carry his bat through a completed Test innings

Bernard Tancred not out 26
South Africa v. England. Cape Town, 26 March 1889

South Africa were introduced to Test cricket with two matches against Major Wharton's touring team in 1889 but were hopelessly outclassed. They lost the First Test by eight wickets and things went from bad to worse when losing the second at Cape Town by an innings and 202 runs.

England batted first and Abel scored the first century in a Test Match in South Africa. With the exception of Tancred the South African batsmen could not cope with the bowling of Briggs who took 7-17 in their first innings and 8-11 in the second. Tancred became the first batsman to carry his bat through a completed Test innings scoring 26 out of a total of 47. There was no improvement in their second innings and South Africa were all out for 43 with even Tancred falling to the lethal Briggs.

Tancred never played Test cricket again, business affairs preventing him from accepting an invitation to visit England with the first South African tourists of 1894.

27

Obstructing the field

Len Hutton obstructing the field 27
England v. South Africa. The Oval, 18 August 1951

Going into the Fifth Test 2-1 against South Africa, England needed only 163 runs in the fourth innings to win in a low scoring game. It looked like openers Hutton and Lawson were going to get all the runs by themselves after scoring 53 in fifty minutes, when suddenly a totally unexpected moment of drama gave South Africa hope of turning the game around and squaring the series.

A ball from spinner Rowan pitched just outside the leg-stump and turned slightly. Hutton got a top-edge and the ball ballooned up head high. Concerned that when the ball fell to the ground it might spin back and hit his stumps, Hutton knocked the ball aside with his bat before it landed. The South African wicket-keeper Endean was preparing to catch the ball but was prevented from doing so by Hutton's reaction. A successful appeal was made but whether the South Africans knew exactly what they were appealing for is not clear. Hutton was not guilty of hitting the ball twice because he was legitimately trying to defend his wicket. The umpires Davies and Chester were in no doubt however, and the scorers were soon advised that Hutton had been given out for the first and only instance in Test cricket of 'Obstructing the Field'.

If Endean had been in a position where he could not reach the ball Hutton would have been entitled to defend his wicket and would not be out. Nor was he guilty of deliberate intention to prevent Endean from catching the ball. But he was guilty of impeding the wicket-keeper by wilful obstruction and so had to go.

May came in next and was out first ball triggering a collapse with England tottering at 90-4. An aggressive 40 from Brown, England's captain, saw them home by four wickets.

28

Going out in style

Arjuna Ranatunga
Sri Lanka v. South Africa. Colombo, 10 August 2000

After 92 Tests and over 5,000 runs, a much-loved legend of Sri Lankan cricket prepared to make his farewell. As an eighteen-year-old schoolboy Ranatunga had played in his country's inaugural Test in 1982, had been in the team that won its first Test Match four and a half years later, taken over as captain in 1989 for a couple of years, returned as captain in 1992 and led his side to its first victory over England in 1993 before going on as captain for a further 56 Tests. He had passed the captaincy to Jayasuriya in July 1999 and when Sri Lanka fielded first in what was to be

Ranatunga's final Test, friends and colleagues formed a guard of honour for his entrance on to the field of play.

In due course Sri Lanka were set a target of 262 runs to win from 68 overs but soon slumped to 37-3. A revival of fortunes by Jaywardine and de Silva took them to 119-4, but any real chance of victory was gone and Ranatunga came in to smack a quick 28 to entertain the crowd before it all ended with a marching band, fanfares and the erection of a stand for formal farewells and emotional applause from a crowd given free entrance for the special moment.

29

Nobody moved

Jack Russell not out 29
England v. South Africa. Jo'burg, 4 December 1995

South Africa declared during the morning of the fourth day of the Second Test, setting England a target of 479. Atherton was still there when Jack Russell joined him just before lunch on the final day, with England 232-5. Few expected England to avoid going 1-0 down in the series. At the start of the partnership everyone was moving around as usual. But as the partnership continued through the afternoon, nerves in the England dressing room were stretched to breaking point with everyone frightened to leave their positions in case any change would bring about the fall of a wicket. After tea, going into the last session, once you were in position you had to stay – whether you needed the loo, whether you needed a drink, bad luck. This was about saving the game for England and nobody moved at all.

The tactics worked and the game was saved, with the Atherton/Russell partnership of 119 unbroken after 75 overs with Jack Russell 29 not out after facing 235 balls.

30

The rock stands firm

Bill Woodfull not out 30
Australia v. England. Brisbane, 5 December 1928

Replying to England's first innings total of 521 Australia lost five wickets for 71, including Bradman playing in his first Test, and crumbled to 122 all out. Despite a lead of 399 England decided to bat again against a depleted Australian attack lacking opening bowler Gregory with cartilage problems. Eventually England declared, the first declaration ever made in a Test played in Australia, and Australia now faced the daunting task of making 742 to win. The fourth day's play ended with Australia 17-1 and to make their task even more difficult, heavy rain fell overnight followed by bright sunshine the next morning with the pitch converted into a classic Brisbane 'sticky'.

It was now that the solid and dependable Bill Woodfull, clergyman's son and schoolmaster, came into his own.

Always difficult to dismiss, his almost non-existent back-lift the basis for pushes forward and deflections, he frustrated the England bowlers while wickets fell at the other end. Missing Kelleway with food poisoning and Gregory who was unable to bat in either innings and never played Test cricket again, Australia were all out for 66 with Woodfull unbeaten and unbowed at 30 not out.

Woodfull's obstinacy throughout the series, including a century at Melbourne that contained only three boundaries, failed to save Australia from losing 4-1. When he was bowled by Hammond in the second innings of the Fifth Test it was the first time his stumps had been hit for over twelve months.

31

Slasher takes his time

Ken Mackay c Evans b Statham
Australia v. England. Lord's, 23 June 1956

Australia were 69-3 in their second innings on day three of the Second Test and only 183 runs ahead when Mackay came to the wicket. Nearly four and a half hours later, after scoring at the rate of seven runs an hour while supporting Benaud in a partnership of 117, Mackay was caught at the wicket for 31 and Australia had a commanding lead of 343. In Australia's first innings he had also been the backbone, while making 38 runs in two and a half hours and his repeat performance in the second innings played a vital part in Australia's victory by 185 runs, inspiring the *Manchester Guardian* to write 'Mackay is like the common cold, there is no cure for that either.'

These were typical innings from 'Slasher' Mackay, who had earned that ironic nickname for his distinctive style of cautious batting with scoring shots restricted to deflections, a sort of shovel stroke of his own invention past mid-wicket, and a half-volley that squirted past cover from an almost non-existent back-lift. His reputation as a match-saver followed a number of rescue acts, but this ignored the enormous contribution his obdurate presence in the middle-order had made to providing a platform for winning matches as well.

32

The birth of the Ashes legend

W.G. Grace c Bannerman b Royle 32
England v. Australia. The Oval, 29 August 1882

The third team of Australian cricketers to tour England only played one Test Match in the summer of 1882, but it was the extraordinary match that led to the creation of the Legend of the Ashes.

Everyone expected England to win and it was with a mixture of disbelief and praise for Australia's victory that the *Wisden Almanac* of 1883 prefaced its report of the match with a comparison of the relevant strengths of the two sides, including batting and bowling averages, to indicate England's overwhelming superiority. So it had been no real surprise when Australia had collapsed all out for 63 in their first innings, but eyebrows had been raised when England fared only a little better by scoring 101. Even so, with a lead of 38 their victory seemed assured. Thanks to a brilliant innings of 55 from Massie Australia managed to get their total into three figures, but that still left England needing a mere 85 runs to win. That target might have been a few runs higher if it had not been for the controversial run-out of Sammy Jones by W.G. Grace. Jones had come in at 99-6 and helped Murdoch raise the score to 110 before Murdoch turned a ball from Steel away on the leg side and the batsmen crossed for a single while the wicket-keeper retrieved the ball and threw it back to Grace who had gone to the stumps. Jones made his ground and turned to move out of his crease to put down a divot on the pitch, believing that Grace had acknowledged his nodded enquiry that the ball was now dead. Grace whipped off the bails instead and appealed for run out. To Jones's disgust the Umpire raised his finger. Spofforth, the Australian fast bowler, came in next, outraged by the actions of Grace, as he himself had been in a position to run out the English batsman Hornby in the first innings for excessive backing-up at the bowler's end, and had only given a warning instead. Even worse, on that occasion Grace had vocally expressed disbelief that the Australian could have even considered taking advantage of such a situation.

When it came time for England to bat, Spofforth was still steaming with rage and took three quick wickets. But Grace was batting brilliantly with 30 out of the 53 runs scored and England seemed set for victory. Even when Grace went to a catch at mid-off and England's run rate dropped to zero during twelve successive overs, England's supporters felt there was no cause for alarm. When another wicket fell only nineteen runs were needed with five wickets in hand but one last effort from Spofforth to take four wickets in nine balls ended England's hopes.

Such was the shock to national pride that an Obituary for English Cricket appeared in the next issue of the *Sporting Times* with the added information that 'The body will be cremated, and the Ashes taken to Australia.' Few appreciated the joke and 'The Decadence of English Cricket' was debated within the columns of every newspaper in the land.

33

Corkie saves the day

Dominic Cork not out 33
England v. West Indies. Lord's, 1 July 2000

The arrival of Dominic Cork on to the international scene in 1995 was one of the most dramatic in Test Match history.

Roaring in from the Nursery End at Lord's to take 7-43 and bowl England to a 72-run victory over the West Indies his were the best figures ever achieved by an Englishman on his debut. And just two matches later Cork grabbed the first hat-trick to be taken by an English bowler in a Test Match since 1957.

Five years later Cork was back at Lord's to play in the 100th Test on that famous ground, once again facing the West Indies. This time his major contribution was with the bat and not the ball. Going in at 140-6, with England needing 48 to win, two more wickets fell and they were still 28 short. Darren Gough came in next, full of encouragement – 'Think how famous we'll be if we score these runs.' Cork steered them to a two-wicket victory with 33 out of the last 51 runs scored, driving Walsh through the covers for the winning boundary – cricket at its very best.

34

Slow but sure

William Scotton b Garrett 34
England v. Australia. Kennington Oval, 12 August 1886

While W.G. Grace was on his way to recapturing the record England Test score with 170, his left-handed opening partner William Scotton assisted him with the highest first wicket stand by either country and a new record for any England wicket.

Scotton's role was to blunt the Australian attack, which included Spofforth. Even Grace made a cautious start, his first 50 taking an unprecedented two hours, but that was nothing compared with Scotton's snail-like progress. He took eighteen overs to get off the mark and after reaching 24 didn't score another run for over an hour. The partnership of 170 ended after nearly four hours and England were on their way to an innings victory and a 3-0 whitewash.

35

17 years later

George Gunn lbw b st Hill 35
England v. West Indies. Barbados, 13 January 1930

Health problems threatened the career of the young George Gunn after a promising start in county cricket, so he took advantage of an opportunity to winter in Australia in 1907/08. His visit coincided with that of the MCC touring team and when the captain, A.O. Jones, fell ill soon after arriving, Gunn was asked to join the party. He seized the chance with both hands and scored a century on his debut in the First Test and added a second in the Fifth. Four years later he was back in Australia with the team that regained the Ashes. There were no centuries this time but an average of 42.3, plus top-scoring with 61 in England's last innings in the final Test, were significant contributions to England's success. On return to the UK the services of Gunn were not required by the selectors during the Triangular Tournament featuring England, South Africa and Australia, and as there were no Tests played in England in 1913, or in the four years of the First World War that followed, by 1918 Gunn's Test career seemed over.

When the first official MCC party went to the West Indies in the winter of 1929/30 they were not expected to meet very stiff opposition and the 50-year-old Gunn, still enjoying enormous success in county cricket, was selected. Going to the wicket in England's first innings in the First Test exactly seventeen years and 316 days since his last Test innings for England at Sydney in 1912, Gunn recorded the longest interval by far between two batsman's innings in Test cricket. The young West Indian player James Sealey making his debut in that same Test had not been born the last time Gunn had batted in a Test Match.

36

New boy makes good

Rodney Hogg c Taylor b Botham 36
Australia v. England. Brisbane, 1 December 1978

Making his debut in the First Test of the series, Hogg came in at 53-7 to join John Maclean, also playing in his first Test Match. Together they took Australia into three figures with a partnership of exactly 50 and Hogg ended with the top score of the innings.

But a total of 116 was never going to be enough, and although Hogg took six wickets in England's first innings, nothing was going to stop England's first victory at Brisbane since 1936. Hogg only got into double figures twice more in the series, his twelve innings realising 59 runs, but he took 41 wickets and was a regular in the Australian Test side for another six years.

37

The tide is turned

Robert Croft not out 37
England v. South Africa. Old Trafford, 6 July 1998

An unbeaten 37 from off-spinner Robert Croft in England's second innings in the Third Test prevented South Africa from taking a 2-0 lead in the series. Going in with six wickets down for 296 and still 72 runs short of preventing an innings defeat with three hours' play left on the final day, the brave resistance of Croft, Gough and, finally, Fraser, against a rampant Donald and Ntini was seen by *Wisden* as a 'Dunkirk style evacuation of the kind much loved of English cricket followers'. England went on to take the series 2-1.

38

Almost the first tie

Sidney Barnes not out 38
England v. Australia. Melbourne, 7 January 1908

Losing the First Test by only two wickets England were anxious to level the series and with a first innings lead of 116 – the right result looked assured. But Australia fought hard and when England were set a target of 282 the game seemed to have swung back in Australia's favour. At the end of the fifth day England were 159-4 and the game poised to go either way. The next morning three wickets fell for a mere 29 runs and Barnes came to the wicket with 84 runs still required.

All seemed lost when Crawford – the last recognised batsman – was out at 209-8, but Humphries joined Barnes and they staged a small revival until Humphries went lbw to Armstrong at 243-9. The Australian captain, Noble, repeatedly changed his bowlers in an attempt to unsettle the batsmen, but Barnes farmed the bowling to protect his new partner, Arthur Fielder. The score grew closer and closer to the target until the two teams were level and the match would have resulted in the first tie in Test Match cricket if Hazlitt – only six yards from the wicket – had run to the stumps after picking up the ball from a tap by Barnes, easily outracing Fielder who'd failed to back up. Instead, the fielder chose to hurl the ball to the wicket-keeper and missed him by yards, as it flew to the boundary while the last England pair desperately crossed for the winning run.

39

Grey power

David Steele b Lillee 39
England v. Australia. Kennington Oval, 30 August 1975

Making his Test Match debut at Lord's against Australia at the age of 33, the grey-haired, bespectacled David Steele delayed his arrival at the wicket after losing his way from the dressing room in the unfamiliar corridors and staircases of the Home of Cricket. Unfazed by the confusion, he went in and scored a half-century and ended the series with an average of 60.83, despite facing Lillee and Thomson at their most dangerous. His gritty determination earned the description 'A bank clerk goes to war' and in the final Test he made top score of 39 out of England's disastrous 191 in reply to 532-8 declared. After England followed-on, Steele again proved his worth by sharing a second-wicket stand of 125 with Edrich. His performances that summer captured the public imagination and he was voted the BBC Sports Personality of the Year.

Steele's first Test century came the following summer against the West Indies and he was the only England batsman to reach double figures in their first innings at Old Trafford, scoring twenty out of 71 in a match they lost by 425 runs. Inexplicably, he was not selected for the next winter tour of India and never played for England again, returning to county cricket as quietly and unobtrusively as he had arrived in the cauldron of Test cricket.

40

Standing firm

Alan Border c Gatting b Embury 40
Australia v. England. Edgbaston, 2 August 1981

Looking to win the Fourth Test at Birmingham to go 2-1 up in the series with a real chance of regaining the Ashes, Australia felt confident going into their second innings needing only 151 runs for victory. At 105-4 everything went wrong for Australia as the next six wickets fell for sixteen runs with Botham taking five of them for one run in 28 balls. In the middle of this debacle Border stood firm with the highest score of the Australian innings in a Test Match in which, for the first time since 1935, no batsman reached a half-century.

Border had made his Test debut two years earlier and had already scored five centuries. He would go on for another thirteen years and when he retired he held the records for most caps, most innings, most runs (11,174), most scores of 50+ (90), most catches in the field, most matches as captain and longest unbroken sequence as a player (153) and as captain (93).

41

'Bodyline' flashpoint

Bill Oldfield retired hurt 41
Australia v. England. Adelaide, 16 January 1933

As the MCC tour of Australia dramatically unfolded in the winter of 1932/33 and the new leg-theory tactics of England's captain, Douglas Jardine, began to take effect, loud complaints were heard from the Australian players, officials, and the Press, who coined the term 'Bodyline'. But loudest of all was the noisy reaction from the crowd that packed the grounds every day. By the time of the Third Test at Adelaide local authorities were concerned that the crowd's disapproval when they saw their heroes being threatened by short-pitched bowling from Larwood and Voce with a packed leg-side field, could take a more aggressive form and turn into a full-scale riot. Four hundred police constables were appointed to make a strong presence in the ground and mounted police were outside. Everyone was aware that violent protests would be dealt with in the strongest possible manner.

The biggest cause for concern was the crowd's potential response to seeing one of their players struck and injured when 'Bodyline' was in operation. There were two flashpoints during the match but fortunately they happened when Larwood was bowling to an orthodox field and neither resulted in the angry demonstrations that had been feared. Instead they triggered a misjudged response from the Australian cricket officials that had a far greater impact upon the future of cricket between Australia and England.

The first occurred on the afternoon of the second day when, at the start of the Australian innings, Woodfull was struck over the heart by a short-pitched ball directed more or less over the middle stump. This was enough to encourage hooting and angry jeering from the crowd, and could have easily grown into the demonstration the officials feared if Woodfull had been hit again after Jardine switched to a 'Bodyline' field. Fortunately there were no more incidents, at least not on the field of play. The England manager, Plum Warner, decided to pay a visit to the Australian dressing room after Woodfull was out, to enquire after his health. Their brief conversation, in which Woodfull was less than complimentary about the English bowling tactics, was leaked to the Press and dramatically featured in Monday morning's newspapers to fuel the flames even further.

Australia were still batting after lunch on the third day and Larwood took the new ball in an attempt to remove Oldfield, the last remaining recognised batsman who was scoring freely. Intending to cut a ball from Larwood, Oldfield changed his mind halfway through the shot and attempted to pull the ball to leg, but only succeeded in deflecting the ball onto his face. Oldfield reeled away from the wicket clutching his head and fell to his knees, soon to be surrounded by concerned players and umpires. Woodfull, an impressive figure of authority wearing a double breasted suit, marched purposefully out to the square and escorted the injured Oldfield back to the pavilion. Woodfull's dignified reaction appears to have satisfied the crowd's need for protest and the feared pitch invasion did not materialise. Oldfield could not return to complete his innings or bat in Australia's second innings. The skull fracture was only an inch away from a spot on his temple, which, had the ball struck there, would almost certainly have resulted in his death.

On the final day of the Test Match the Australian Cricket Board sent a cable to the MCC in London protesting at the England bowling tactics and calling them 'unsportsmanlike'. All hell broke loose and not only the relationship between the two cricketing bodies but diplomatic relations at the highest government level between Australia and England were seriously endangered.

It was all sorted out in the end but even after 76 years the scars still remain.

42

Australia Day blues

Tim May not out 42
Australia v. West Indies. Adelaide, 26 January 1993

Australia began the fourth day of the Fourth Test needing only 186 runs to win, a victory that would put them 2-0 up in the Series and give them the Frank Worrell Trophy to add to the country's annual celebrations of Australia Day. It ended with West Indies levelling the Series with victory by 1 run, the narrowest victory ever achieved in the previous 116 years of Test Match cricket.

A stunned crowd were shocked into silence when the last Australian wicket fell. Only seconds before, the sound of 'Waltzing Matilda' had resounded around the ground as the home supporters began early celebrations in anticipation of seeing the two runs needed being added to the score. Few had expected to see Australia in such a winning position after their first eight wickets had fallen for only 102 runs, but a determined stand between Justin Langer, making his Test debut, and Tim May batting with an injured hand, had taken Australia to within 42 runs of their target. It still seemed too much to ask of the last pair but May and last man McDermott edged the score closer until McDermott failed to avoid a lifting ball from Walsh and gloved it to the wicket-keeper just two runs short. May had also played an important part the previous day in keeping the West Indies lead within reach by taking five wickets for five runs in 32 balls.

43

From start to finish

Billy Zulch not out 43
South Africa v. England. Cape Town, 12 March 1910

Already 3-1 up in the series, an overconfident South Africa crashed all out for 103 in reply to England's 417 with Billy Zulch becoming the second South African to carry his bat through a completed innings against England. Zulch toured Australia the following winter scoring two centuries but was unavailable to visit England for the Triangular Tournament in 1912 and his sixteen Test appearances were ended by the outbreak of the First World War in 1914.

44

Anchor man

'Polly' Umrigar not out 44
India v. West Indies. Calcutta, 3 January 1958

After 24 attempts in twenty years India won her first Test Match against England at Madras in 1952 with a debut century from Umrigar. India travelled to England four months later with high hopes but came up against Freddie Trueman making his debut as England's new fast bowler and he blew them away with 29 wickets in the four Tests, including 8-31 at Old Trafford. Umrigar fared no better than the rest with 43 runs from seven innings but on return to India he came back strongly with a century against Pakistan and then two more centuries on the tour of West Indies the following year.

India were no match for the West Indies when they came to India in 1958/59 and the visitors were already 1-0 ahead in the Series by the Third Test at Calcutta. In reply to 614-5 declared India were all out for 124. Going in at 52-3 Umrigar put up stiff resistance and scored 44 out of the next 72 runs to remain unbeaten, although his efforts were in vain as India went on to lose by an innings and 336 runs.

Once again, Umrigar's form fluctuated and during the 1959/60 tour of Australia he was dropped for the last two Tests after scoring 52 runs from five innings. He was brought back against Pakistan in 1960/61 when he scored three centuries during five drawn Tests. On retirement in 1962 Umrigar had scored more runs for India than any other countryman, including twelve centuries, in his 59 Tests.

45

Unbeaten century

Alan Border not out 45
Australia v. England. Sydney, 11 January 1979

Weakened by a virus and heat exhaustion England were bundled out for 152 and at lunch on the second day Australia at 126-1 seemed to be heading to an easy victory with a good chance of regaining the Ashes with only two more Tests remaining. But the determined English bowlers restricted Australia's lead to only 142 and that might have been even less without Border's unbeaten 60. Despite Boycott going to the first ball of their second innings England fought back to overtake the Australian lead and thanks to a magnificent 150 from Randall in just under ten hours of intense concentration, reached 346 leaving Australia with a target of 205 in four and a half hours.

Only the sure defence of Border could cope with the spinning partnership of Embury and Miller bowling with the attacking fields set by England's captain Brearley. But nothing the future Australian captain could do would prevent England from retaining the Ashes – the first time since 1954/55. Finishing not out for the second time in the match with 45 runs out of the 111 scored, and actually having compiled an unbeaten century in the match, Border demonstrated, in what was only his second Test Match, that he was in a class of his own and certain to be a thorn in England's side for years to come.

46

Running riot

Ajit Wadekar c McKenzie b Stackpole 46
India v. Australia. Bombay, 8 November 1969

The Australian tour of India in the winter of 1969/70 was a bad-tempered affair with disagreements over umpire decisions and crowd demonstrations turning into full-scale riots. It all kicked off during the very first Test at Bombay, when local favourite Venkataraghavan – only playing because public outcry against his omission had been satisfied by the withdrawal of the selector's original choice – was given out, caught at the wicket, with India going to 114-8 in their second innings and only 40 runs in front. Venkataraghavan's partner, Wadekar, had gone in earlier at 56-4 and was desperately trying to shore up the Indian innings and give Australia a real target in the final innings.

Wadekar managed to ignore the riot that threatened to stop play during the last hour of the fourth day, but even his top score of the innings could not prevent an easy eight-wicket victory for Australia, who went on to win the Series 2-1.

47

The start of another blackwash

David Gower b Walsh 47
England v. West Indies. Trinidad, 9 March 1986

After losing all five Tests in a home Series against West Indies eighteen months earlier England, under Gower's captaincy, were hoping for a good start in the First Test of their tour of the Islands in 1986. Gower top-scored with 66 out of England's 176 in their first innings, including a century partnership with Allan Lamb, but England started their second innings before lunch on the third day 223 runs behind. They immediately lost Slack with only two runs on the board and Gower came in with pressure on him again to play a captain's innings. A partnership of 80 with Gooch gave England some hope of a revival but after Gower was out, bowled by a shooter from Walsh, the wickets began to tumble and Gower's 47 was top score out 315, the highest Test innings total in which no batsman reached 50.

West Indies won the Series 5-0, their second successive 'blackwash', in which England never achieved a first innings lead against the lethal bowling of Marshall, Garner, Patterson and Walsh.

48

Fatal decision

Ravi Shastri not out 48
India v. Australia. Madras, 22 September 1986

Starting the First Test of a Series of three in India, Australia made an impressive beginning with a first innings total of 547-7 declared, including a double century from Jones and centuries from Boon and Border. When India managed to avoid the follow-on, Border cut short the Australian second innings at the start of the final day's play and set India the difficult, but not impossible, task of making 348 to win. By tempting India to go for the target Border had hopes that his spin bowlers, who had taken seven of the Indian first innings wickets, would bowl Australia to victory. But with all the Indian top-order batsmen making runs, at 331-6 it looked as if Border had seriously miscalculated. Then Bright answered his captain's prayers with three wickets for the addition of only thirteen runs and last man Maninder Singh joined Shastri with four runs needed to win.

One of the great all-rounders of Indian cricket Shastri had come in at 252-5 and was steering India comfortably home when the collapse had occurred. Now he found himself facing the last three balls of the match with the desperate choice of either hitting-out for the two runs needed for victory, or taking a single to be sure of avoiding defeat. He chose the latter and hoped that his new partner could scramble another all-important single. With the fifth ball of the last over Greg Matthews struck Maninder on the pads to give a clear lbw decision. The result was only the second tie in the 1,052 Test Matches that had been played since 1877.

49

One short of the record

George Mann not out 49
England v. New Zealand. Headingley, 14 June 1949

In the mistaken belief that the quality of the New Zealand touring team visiting England in the summer of 1949 only justified Test Matches of three days' duration, all four Tests were drawn without a result in sight.

At least England's captain, George Mann back from leading a successful team to South Africa, showed some imagination with attempts to give his players a fighting chance of victory. In the First Test Mann could have set a new record for the fastest half-century in Test Match cricket, but declared the innings closed after scoring 49 in 25 minutes. His sacrifice gave his bowlers time for 49 overs to bowl New Zealand out with plenty of runs to play with, even in the unlikely case of them going for the target of 298 runs. There was nothing in the wicket to help the bowlers and the game petered out to a draw.

In the Second Test at Lord's, Mann made history by declaring on the first day, mistakenly taking advantage of an experimental Law allowing first day declarations in all three day matches but not realising that this did not apply to Test Matches. But it was to no avail as his bowlers again failed to get a breakthrough in the fifteen minutes left for play.

50

The score that came before

Ian Botham c Marsh b Lillee 50
England v. Australia. Leeds, 18 July 1981

Everyone remembers Botham's brilliant 149 not out in England's second innings at Leeds in 1981, but who remembers his half-century in the first innings?

Going into the Ashes series of 1981 England had not won a Test Match since beating India at Bombay seventeen months earlier, and they immediately went 1-0 down to Australia at Trent Bridge. The Second Test at Lord's was drawn and when Botham went in at 87-5 at Leeds in reply to Australia's 401-9 declared in which Botham had already made herculean efforts to take 6-95 from 39.2 overs, the series seemed as good as lost. Botham's response was to attack the bowling of Lillee, Alderman and Lawson with an aggressive 50 that included eight fours, and ended with top score out of 174. It was not enough to stave off the follow-on but without it, England's successful attempt to make Australia bat again would have been that much more difficult. As it was, the final target of 130 appeared easy enough until Willis demolished the Australian second innings with 8-43, and England won by eighteen runs. It was the narrowest margin in an Ashes Test since 1928/29 and the first victory in the twentieth century by a team that followed on – and only the second such result in Test cricket.

As brilliant as Botham's second innings undoubtedly was, it would have counted for nothing without those 50 runs two days earlier.

51

The Tiger goes down fighting

Arjuna Ranatunga c & b Bracewell 51
Sri Lanka v. New Zealand. Kandy, 14 March 1984

Sri Lanka were feeling optimistic when New Zealand set them a target of 263 to win with 130 minutes and an extra twenty overs available. Everything went wrong from the start, when Hadlee took four wickets for eight runs in the first six overs. The collapse was a huge disappointment for the large Sri Lankan crowd and riot police were called to the ground.

Ranatunga had entered at 14-4, but before he could settle in, two more wickets fell and Sri Lanka were 18-6 and heading for the lowest score in Test Match history. The crowd's jeers soon turned to cheers as Ranatunga cracked 51 runs from 45 balls, but when he went at 97-8 it was all over and the riot police were back in business.

Sri Lanka's 97 was the lowest innings total to include an individual half-century and in which all eleven players had batted.

52

Playing the percentages

Asanka Gurusinha not out 52
Sri Lanka v. India. Chandigarh, 24 and 25 November 1990

India were playing their first home Test Match for two years as part of a short and hastily arranged tour of one Test Match and three one-day internationals by Sri Lanka. During their absence India had been on four separate tours abroad and played fourteen Tests without a win. Political unrest provoked a late transfer of the Test Match from Jullundur to Chandigar and India selected three spin-bowlers to take advantage of what was expected to be an under-prepared pitch.

At first the wicket played well and India reached 208-3 with little difficulty but then were spun out for under 300. Sri Lanka began well until Raju came on to bowl at 50-2 and then lost five wickets for two runs in 39 balls. At the end of the second day Sri Lanka were 75-8 with Gurusinha 47 not out, and the next morning continued still needing fourteen runs to avoid the follow-on. The last two wickets fell for the addition of only seven runs and batting again Sri Lanka never looked like avoiding an innings defeat. Gurusinha's magnificent effort in the first innings had lasted three hours while facing 159 balls and his score of 52 was the highest percentage of a completed innings total under 100.

53

Top score twice

Neil Harvey c Dexter b Trueman 53
Australia v. England. Headingley, 8 July 1961

Neil Harvey played one of his finest innings in what will always be remembered as 'Trueman's Match'. The England fast bowler had taken 11 wickets for 88 runs to help England win the Third Test by eight wickets and square the series.

The Australian left-hander had actually top-scored with 73 out of Australia's first innings of 237 before coming to the wicket in the second innings at 4-1 still trailing England by 58 runs. The arrears were eventually cleared with the loss of only one more wicket and at 98-2, with Harvey again batting superbly well, Australia looked in a strong position.

The return of Trueman to the attack began a procession of Australian victims despite resistance from Harvey, the only Australian batsman to reach a half-century, and with five wickets falling to Trueman from 24 deliveries without conceding a run – England were on course for victory.

54

Victory in the last over

'Cec' Pepper not out 54
Australia v. England. Lord's, 22 May 1945

Following the announcement of VE Day on 8 May 1945 to celebrate the Allied victory over Germany in the Second World War, it was decided to extend a series of one-day games arranged to be played between England and an Australian Services Team up to three-day 'Victory Test' matches. They produced such spectacular cricket, and were so popular with a public starved of such epic struggles for six years, that it seems appropriate just this once to go outside those innings played in full Test Matches, and make an exception for an innings that sums up the whole attitude of players who wanted only to entertain throughout that joyful summer.

On the third day of the first 'Victory' Test Match Australia required 107 runs to win with only 70 minutes left for play. When the last over arrived five runs were still needed and Pepper, who had walloped more than half of the runs required, including a ball in the previous over into the Grandstand boxes for six, saw Australia home to an eight-wicket victory. Five 'Victory' Tests were played in all, with honours appropriately shared at 2-2 and one match drawn.

55

First in last out

Desmond Haynes c & b Cairns 55
West Indies v. New Zealand. Dunedin,
8, 9, 10, 12 and 13 Feb 1980

On the first day of the First Test of a three-match series, the ball kept exceptionally low and only Haynes, who had opened the innings, consistently got onto the front foot to make top score out of the West Indies total of 140, being last man out after four and a half hours of concentrated batting.

West Indies began their second innings 109 runs behind at the end of the second day and at one stage it looked as if they would lose by an innings. Once again Haynes came to the rescue, refusing to be dislodged while taking part in stands of 88 with King and 63 with Murray to give West Indies a fighting chance. Early on the morning of the fifth day, Haynes was last out again, having batted right through the innings for a second time to score 105 in just over seven hours. He had become the first man to bat throughout both innings of a Test Match, but his efforts proved to be in vain when New Zealand grabbed victory by one wicket in the last over of the match. Haynes was unable to field during the New Zealand second innings and missed the chance of becoming the first player from West Indies to be on the field every day of a Test Match.

56

Five boundaries

David Hookes c Fletcher b Underwood 56
Australia v. England. Centenary Test at Melbourne,
14 March 1977

Hookes forced his way into the Australian team by scoring five centuries in six innings over a period of only seventeen days playing for South Australia in Sheffield Shield matches. Less than a month later, still only aged 21, he was walking out to bat on the first day of what was one of the most famous cricket matches to be played in the twentieth century.

His innings did not last very long, but neither did those of any of the other Australian batsmen, and the whole team was out for 138. As bad as that total was, England's first was even worse and Australia started again with an unexpected lead of 43. Struggling to reach 132 with four wickets down, Australia had high hopes that Hookes would turn the game around in their favour. Determined not to let them down, he immediately set about the bowling of Tony Greig and with supreme confidence drove the bowling of the England captain past helpless fieldsmen for five consecutive boundaries. In partnership with Walters an Australian revival was in full swing and although Hookes went for 56 they were eventually in a position to declare and win the match by 45 runs.

57

Patience is a virtue

Rusi Modi not out 57
India v. England. Lord's, 22 June 1946

When England took the field at the start of the Test against India in 1946 it was almost seven years since the last Test Match had been played at Lord's following the interruption of the Second World War. The stands were packed and hundreds were allowed to overflow and sit covering every available blade of grass between the boundary ropes and the picket fences. Nobody cared that the cricket itself was slow and everyone appreciated the outstanding patience and determination of the tall and thin Indian batsman who had gone in at 44-3 and remained strong and resolute as wickets fell at the other end, seven of them to Alec Bedser on his Test Match debut.

58

Legends are made of this

George Hirst not out 58
England v. Australia. Kennington Oval, 13 August 1902

England had already lost the series but her victory in the final Test at the Oval in 1902 is part of cricket legend.

At the end of the second day Australia were 255 runs ahead with two wickets in hand. A heavy dew overnight made the wicket almost unplayable before lunch and the last two Australian wickets fell for only seven runs, followed by the loss of five England wickets for 48. Then Jackson was joined by Jessop and a recovery looked possible, although when lunch was taken England were 87-5 and still 176 runs short of victory. In the afternoon the English pair continued their partnership and added 109 runs before Jackson went after an hour and forty minutes batting for his 49. Now George Hirst came in to join Jessop who continued on his way to a glorious century, ending with 104 runs out of the 139 runs made during the 77 minutes he was at the crease facing 80 balls. England were still 76 runs short and now Hirst took over the responsibility of trying to steer them home for an unexpected victory, first with a partnership of 27 with Lockwood and then 34 with Lilley. Last man Rhodes came in at 248-9, still fifteen runs short. The next 36 balls were bowled with every England supporter on the edge of their seats as they edged nearer their target. Another fourteen runs came from eight singles, a boundary and another single converted into a couple by an overthrow, and the scores were level.

Trumble had bowled unchanged from the Pavilion End from 11.30am until 4pm and it was from his 203rd ball of the innings that an off-drive from Rhodes gave England the winning run, with the crowd cheering itself hoarse at what would become a legendary result.

59
Starting the way you mean to go on

Herbert Sutcliffe c V. Richardson b Mailey 59
England v. Australia. Sydney, 20 and 22 December 1924

The famous opening partnership of Hobbs and Sutcliffe started with a century stand of 136 in the summer of 1924 against South Africa. It almost ended before it began when Sutcliffe was lucky to escape an easy run-out with only eight runs on the board. No England supporter would like to contemplate what their chances would have been of winning back the Ashes in 1926, and then retaining them in Australia in 1928/29 if these two openers had not blended together right from the start. They walked out together to open an England innings on no fewer than 38 occasions and in fifteen of those they were not parted until the score had gone past three figures.

In the first innings of the First Test in Sydney in 1924, they opened against Australia for the first time and gave

England a great start with a stand of 157, broken into almost two equal halves by the Sunday rest day. Sutcliffe, who was the first to go, contributed 59, while Hobbs went on to a personal century. Ten more three figure partnerships against Australia were to follow before they ended at the Oval in 1930 with Hobbs retiring from Test cricket at the age of 47.

60

Battlefield survivor

Mohinder Amarnath st Murray b Jumadeen 60
India v. West Indies. Kingston, 25 April 1976

India started the match on a recently relaid pitch, which developed unpredictable bounce at both ends once the openers had made a solid century partnership. Holding began to bang the ball down short with frightening results. Gaekwad was hit on the head and spent the next three days in hospital, Viswanath had a finger fractured and took no further part in the match, and Patel had to have stitches after a ball cut his mouth open. When six wickets had fallen, India's captain Bedi declared the innings closed in order to protect himself and Chandrasekhar from injury and be available to bowl. India did not have fast bowlers to consider any sort of retaliation and needed 125 overs from their spin bowlers to keep the West Indies first innings lead to only 85 runs.

With three men absent and both Bedi and Chandrasekhar unable to bat, claiming hand injuries sustained while fielding, India were reduced to just six batsmen in their second innings. Gavaskar went with only five runs on the board and Amarnath and Vengsarkar, batting with great courage, put on 63 for the second wicket. Amarnath continued with Madan Lal to add 31 for the third before going at 97-3 and when two more wickets fell without any change to the score, the innings ended: not with a declaration as was first believed, but for the simple reason that there was no one else fit enough to bat.

61

Captain courageous

Imran Khan c & b Gray 61
Pakistan v. West Indies. Faisalabad, 24 October 1986

Pakistan had not beaten the West Indies in a Test Match for over 9 years when they began a new series in 1986. To add to the West Indian confidence they arrived in Pakistan after a sequence of seven consecutive Test Match victories.

The events of the first morning of the First Test gave Pakistan little hope of being able to reverse the trend after they had collapsed to 37-5. It seemed business as usual for Viv Richards and his team but Pakistan's new captain came to the wicket with other ideas. Imran first joined Salim

Malik in a half-century partnership until it ended when the West Indian pace quartet claimed another victim and Salim Malik had his arm broken just above the wrist. Imran refused to be intimidated and carried on to a last wicket partnership of 39 with Tamseef Ahmed.

Eventually Pakistan were able to restrict the West Indian first innings lead to under three figures and they were encouraged to keep fighting and set a final target of 240. Imran continued to play the captain's part by taking the first two wickets, with only sixteen runs on the board and the spin of Qadir with 6-16 saw Richards and Co. bundled out for their lowest Test score of 53.

62

Last man top score

Albert Vogler not out 62
South Africa v. England. Cape Town, 31 March 1906

Albert Vogler came to England in 1905 with the ambition to qualify for Middlesex by working as a professional on the ground staff at Lord's. He played a few games for the MCC with some success and was then asked to return to South Africa to play in the five Test series against Plum Warner's MCC touring side. The South African selectors took the unusual step of naming an unchanged side for all five Tests and against an only average England team the strategy worked well as they won 4-1.

Vogler's contribution as a leg-break bowler and tail-end batsman was only average until the final Test. Going in at 239-9 he was in a stand of 94 with Sherwell, which put South Africa 146 runs in front and in a position to win by an innings. Vogler's 62 was the highest score by a No. 11 batsman in Test Matches and remained the record for 67 years.

63

Defiance

Lionel Tennyson c Gregory b McDonald 63
England v. Australia. Headingley, 4 July 1921

Under the leadership of Johnny Douglas England had lost seven Tests in a row against Australia and a new captain was appointed for the Third Test of the 1921 series. The Honourable Lionel Tennyson had already played six Tests under the captaincy of Douglas, five in South Africa and the Second Test of 1921 at Lord's where he had made an undefeated 74 in the second innings trying to save England from another defeat. Taking over as captain was a popular choice and Douglas was content to play under him.

Everything went wrong from the start of the first day of the match. Tennyson had his left hand split between thumb and forefinger while fielding and needed four stitches, then Hobbs was taken ill with appendicitis in the afternoon and would take no further part in the match.

By midday on the second day England had collapsed to 67-5 in reply to Australia's 407. A spirited retaliation from Douglas and Brown took them to 164, but when two more wickets fell, England were still 91 short of saving the follow-on, with neither Hobbs nor Tennyson able to bat. Or so everyone believed until Tennyson was seen coming onto the field padded-up with his left hand heavily bandaged. Patriotic cheering rang around the ground as the crowd recognised the brave, but perhaps nothing more than brief, gesture of defiance.

Brave it certainly was, brief it was not. For 80 minutes Tennyson, batting with his right hand only, defied the Australian bowlers by getting quickly into position to drive whenever possible and scoring 63 out of 106 runs including eight fours from the pace bowling of Gregory and McDonald. He had taken England past the follow-on target and eventually returned to the pavilion to a hero's welcome.

Despite Tennyson coming out again to score 36 in England's second innings the result was always going to be in Australia's favour, but his outstanding leadership saw something of a recovery in England's fortunes in the remaining two Tests, both drawn but with England on top at the end. It would be another five years before England found another captain of such character in Percy Chapman to inspire them to win back the Ashes.

64

Going for a win

Kim Hughes not out 64
Australia v. India. Calcutta, 30 and 31 October 1979

Going into the Fifth Test, a weakened Australia, following mass defections to Packer's World Series Cricket, were one game down and looking to level the series as a platform for a decider in the sixth and final Test at Bombay.

A first innings lead of only 95 with less than two days left for play put pressure on Australia to make quick runs if they were to secure the result they needed. Losing five wickets for 81 runs by the end of the fourth day looked to have turned the game in India's favour.

Determined to go for the win at all cost, Kim Hughes, Australia's naïve but refreshingly courageous 25-year-old captain in only his eleventh Test launched into an all-out attack and Australia added 70 runs in 72 minutes. It was his innings that gave Hughes the opportunity to make a brave but desperate declaration when he asked India to make 247 runs in just over four hours. Any chance of help from the pitch on the last day was squeezed out by the heavy roller and it was a gamble that could only have come off if India's batsmen self-destructed. At 70-3 with Gavaskar, Vengsarkar and Viswanath back in the pavilion, the hopes of Hughes and his team were high but Sharma swung the match back in India's favour before time ran out and the match ended as an unsatisfactory draw.

65

A leader is found

Imran Khan b Miller 65
Pakistan v. England. Edgbaston, 1 August 1982

Imran Khan made his debut for Pakistan in 1971 and was in and out of the side until becoming a prominent figure in Kerry Packer's World Series Cricket between 1977 and 1979. Returning to international Test Match cricket, he made his first Test century against West Indies in 1980 and was a natural choice as leader of the team to tour England in 1982. It would prove a wise decision, but in the First Test he was required to make his mark as an inspirational captain who led by example. Taking seven wickets for 52 runs in England's first innings, he saw his team fail to take advantage of his magnificent effort and they started the fourth day needing 313 runs to win.

Pakistan had collapsed to 66-5 when Imran came to the wicket and although his top score of 65 helped double the innings total England eventually cruised home by 113 runs. But the pattern had been set and while completing a Test Match career that included six centuries, eighteen half-centuries and a record for Pakistan of 362 wickets, Imran led Pakistan in twelve series after 1982, winning four, drawing six, and losing only to Australia in 1983/84 and 1989/90.

66

Three top scores in a row

David Gower c Dujon b Marshall 66
England v. West Indies. Barbados, 22 and 23 March 1986

After top scoring in both innings of the Second Test (see
47) Gower went straight on to do it all over again in the first
innings of the Third Test. Gooch and Gower took England
to 110-1 by close of play on the second day. But the next
morning they collapsed all out for 189 and followed on
229 behind. Brilliant bowling by the West Indies quartet
of Marshall, Garner, Patterson and Holding won the game
by an innings, England's eighth consecutive defeat by the
West Indies.

67

First to carry his bat

John Barrett not out 67
Australia v. England. Lord's, 22 and 23 July 1890

Medical studies kept John Barrett out of top-class cricket
until selected to visit England with the 1890 Australian
tourists. He played in his first Test at Lord's and scored 67
in the second innings out of 176 after being promoted to
opener and became the first player to carry his bat through
a completed innings in a Test Match between England and

Australia. One more Test at the Oval completed Barrett's Test Match career before he began work as a doctor on his return home to Australia.

68

The Barnacle

Trevor Bailey b Mackay 68
England v. Australia. Brisbane, 8 and 9 December 1958

England arrived in Australia determined to keep the Ashes won five years before, but it all started badly and they never took a first innings lead throughout the series, which they lost 4-0.

Always on the defensive, at least England supporters thought they could expect a gritty resistance from Bailey, who relished a crisis and would fight to the bitter end whatever the Australians threw at him. So it proved in the second innings of the First Test at Brisbane when England started 52 runs behind and lost Richardson with only 28 on the board prompting May to promote Bailey from number six to first wicket down. While other wickets fell around him, Bailey put up a brick wall to the Australian attack, taking just under six hours to reach 50 off 350 balls – the slowest recorded half-century in all first-class cricket. Not satisfied with that, Bailey batted on for a further hour and 38 minutes to reach 68 at a final average for the innings of nine runs an hour. Out of the 425 balls he personally faced, he scored from only 40, including only four boundaries. It was not enough and England lost by eight wickets.

On the strength of his defensive qualities, Bailey was moved up to open the innings for the rest of the series, an experiment that had been tried from time to time before with mixed success. This time it proved a failure. The highest partnership was 30 and in five of the seven opening partnerships either Bailey or his partner was dismissed with fewer than double figures on the board. In the final Test Bailey went for a duck in both innings and never played for England again.

69

Lower order fireworks

Michael Holding c Willis b Pringle 69
West Indies v. England. Edgbaston, 16 June 1984

On the morning of the third day of the First Test of the 1984 series, West Indies were already 264 runs in front of England's first innings when Holding joined Baptiste at 455-8. The home team, their confidence already damaged after returning from winter tours to New Zealand and Pakistan where they had lost both series, expected the last two West Indian wickets to fall quickly so that they could at least hope to make an attempt to save the match. It was not to be so easy and the situation was going to get a great deal worse.

261

Holding and Baptiste set about attacking the weary bowlers and rattled up another 150 runs in just under two hours, a ninth-wicket Test record for West Indies against England. Baptiste ended with an unbeaten 87 while Holding hit four sixes and eight fours to reach his highest Test score of 69 from only 80 balls.

West Indies went on to win by an innings and eventually take the series 5-0, the first 'blackwash' in England.

70

Double figures for everyone

Mohinder Amarnath b O'Sullivan 70
India v. New Zealand. Kanpur, 18 November 1976

India's 524-9 declared at Kanpur in 1976 is the highest total in Test cricket in which no batsman scored a century, but in which all eleven batsmen reached double figures. And the highest individual score in that innings was 70 by Mohinder Amarnath going in at first wicket down.

71

The Watson-Bailey epic

Trevor Bailey c Benaud b Ring 71
England v. Australia. Lord's, 30 June 1953

Another rearguard action from 'The Barnacle' (see 68), but this time one that saved the match for England and set the tone for the eventual recovery of the Ashes.

On the afternoon of the third day England had looked to be in a commanding position at 279-2 in reply to Australia's 346. The next eight wickets fell for 93 runs giving only a slender lead, which Australia soon knocked off and then advanced steadily to challenge England with a target of 343 to win. England began their second innings with only 60 minutes of play left on the fourth day and all seemed lost when Kenyon, Hutton and Graveney all went for only twelve runs, ending the day at 20-3. Few expected the game to last beyond 3pm of the next afternoon, others pessimistically forecasted that it would be all over by lunch. But at least Compton was now batting well and Watson was still there from the night before. They added 53 to the total to give a glimmer of hope for an unexpected victory, but Compton went and Bailey came to the wicket with nearly five hours of play remaining. A draw was all England could hope for now, all thoughts of winning forgotten.

Bailey's highest score against Australia in nine previous innings had been 15, but at least there was no pressure upon him to score runs in this situation. Stubborn defence was all that was required from him now, while Watson at the other end could continue with his calm and classic style to frustrate the Australian bowlers. The luncheon interval came and went with no further loss of wickets and at 3pm the Australian captain Hassett took the new ball for those destroyers of England batting in the three previous Ashes series – Lindwall and Miller. Bailey was struck twice on the hand by rising balls but ignored the pain, which only inspired him to even more dogged defence while ten new ball overs produced only nine runs. At tea Watson and Bailey were still together and the crowd, which had grown in numbers as word went around that England were still fighting for a draw, began to believe in the impossible. At 5.30 Watson completed his century but twenty minutes later was caught at short-leg and the partnership of 193 runs was over. Then Bailey went at 246-6 after batting 257 minutes for his 71 and England supporters held their breath as it suddenly seemed possible that the supreme effort of Watson and Bailey might have all been in vain and Australia would grab a last-minute victory. But first Brown and then Evans and Wardle saw England safely home.

72

Last chance for glory

'Foffie' Williams c Evans b Howarth 72
West Indies v. England. Barbados, 24 January 1948

Some fierce hitting by 'Foffie' Williams in West Indies' second innings in their first Test Match since the Second World War turned the tide and gave them a commanding lead. He had gone in at 144-5 when it looked like England had made a breakthrough and might face an easy target in the last innings of the match. In one hour at the wicket 'Foffie' changed everything. He reached his half-century in 30 minutes and went on to 72, which included two sixes and two fours off the first four balls of an over from Laker. West Indies were able to declare at 351-9 and it almost worked when England collapsed to 86-4 chasing 395 to win, but a tropical storm on the last morning prevented any further play.

73

Fastest fifty

Kapil Dev c & b Sarfraz 73
India v. Pakistan. Karachi, 23 December 1982

Every time Kapil Dev went in to the wicket he looked likely to break the record for the fastest Test Match century in terms of deliveries received. He came close to it on more than one occasion while scoring eight centuries in his Test career, while three of his twenty-seven half centuries appear in the top six of the fastest fifties in terms of fewest balls. And all this while taking 434 wickets as India's premier strike bowler.

His heroic efforts did not always guarantee India victory and at Karachi in 1982 he went in at 70-5, attempting to stop the rot with his usual style of blistering attack. He reached 50 in 30 minutes to achieve the Test Match record and went on to 73 off only 54 balls to see the total reach 169. It was never going to be enough and India were beaten by an innings.

74

Not a day goes by

'Jai' Jaisimha b Mackay 74
India v. Australia. Calcutta,
23, 24, 25, 27 and 28 January 1960

Jaisimha had only played in one Test in England during India's tour of England the previous summer, and was given a second chance in the last Test against Australia when the selectors were looking to strengthen the lower order in the hopes of squaring the series. He could not have expected to be so totally involved in the match when he became the first batsman to bat on every day of a five-day match.

Going in at 142-7 he was two not out at the close of play on the first day and remained unbeaten on twenty when the Indian innings closed next morning. India started their second innings on the third day 137 runs behind and after two wickets had fallen for 67 Jaisimha was sent in as nightwatchman. He batted all the next day to reach 59 and was not out until the fifth and final day for 74. As a result India were able to set Australia a target of 203 in two and a half hours, which was declined and the game ended as a draw, a better result than India could have expected without the stirling contribution from Jaisimha

Jaisimha's ability to stay at the wicket continued with his next Test innings, against Pakistan at Kanput, when he broke the record for fewest runs scored in a complete day, making 49 not out of his final total of 99, ironically brought to an end when attempting a quick single to reach three figures. With that sort of stubborn determination it is not surprising that Jaisimha went on to establish himself as a regular in the Indian Test team and played in another 37 Tests making three centuries and ending with an average of 30.68.

75

Highest score by number eleven

Zaheer Khan st Khaled Maslud b Mohammad Ashraful 75
India v. Bangladesh. Dhaka, 12 December 2004

With two of India's greatest players, Tendulkar and Kumble, both chasing records, the result of the first Test of India's first ever tour of Bangladesh was never in any real doubt. On the first day Kumble broke Kapil Dev's record of 434 wickets for India, and on the second day Tendulkar equalled Gavaskar's world record of 34 Test centuries.

An unexpected record was also achieved by Zaheer Khan after going in at 393-9 and adding 133 runs for the last wicket with Tendulkar, who by now was into his double century. Khan's 75 is the highest Test score by a number eleven batsman and included ten fours and two sixes.

76

Lord Ted shows the way

Ted Dexter c Grout b Benaud 76
England v. Australia. Old Trafford, 1 August 1961

Going into the Fourth Test tied at one win each, the destination of the Ashes was wide open in the summer of 1961. Rain delayed the start of play on the first day until the afternoon and then Australia crashed all out for 190.

The wicket improved on the second day but England could only crawl to 187-3 with Dexter already out for sixteen when trying to hit himself out of a poor run of scores since a brilliant 180 in the First Test. By tea on the third day England had reached 361-7 when ex-England captain Walter Robins stormed into the England dressing room and demanded a change of tactics. He and many others were concerned that England's lethargic approach to scoring runs in recent years had seen them drop down to the bottom of the list of countries playing enterprising and entertaining cricket. Robins lacked any real authority but was a respected figure, and while there is no evidence that his opinion had any influence – except perhaps on Dexter, when England came to their second innings – after play resumed the last three England wickets fell for only six runs as the tail-enders tried to hurry the score along. Australia took hope from this good fortune and knocked off the deficit of 177 runs for the loss of only two wickets.

When the Australian second innings ended on the fifth and final day England were left with 230 minutes to score 256 runs to win. Everyone recognised that if anyone was going to swing the game England's way, it would have to be the swashbuckling Dexter. The opening pair put together a very useful 40 – at a run a minute – before being parted, and Dexter arrived in the middle with the stage set for a dramatic climax to the match. He did not disappoint and immediately started by lashing the Australian bowlers to all corners of the field. England reached 150-1 and seemed home and dry when the Australian skipper, Benaud, switched to round the wicket and bowling into the rough, in an attempt to tie Dexter down. Going for a square cut off a ball, which turned and lifted, Dexter edged it straight to the wicket-keeper. His 76 had come in 85 minutes, including fourteen fours and one six, and he was cheered back into the pavilion by England supporters certain that victory was theirs for the taking, with only 106 runs needed at a run a minute with eight wickets in hand. Whether it was the Robins influence or not, it is certain that, in their determination to win as quickly as possible, the remaining England batsmen were undisciplined and suffered from a complete lack of control as the wickets fell, and they were soon all out, 55 runs short. The chance to regain the Ashes was lost and England's captain, Peter May, resigned at the end of the series. Dexter accepted the invitation to take over but was never able to regain the Ashes as hoped, although he did restore pride in a more positive England Test team, winning nine and only losing seven of the 30 Tests in which he was captain.

77

Saving the follow-on with sixes

Kapil Dev not out 77
India v. England. Lord's, 28 and 29 July 1990

In a brilliant Test Match memorable for a treble century from Gooch, his 333 the highest Test score at Lord's, plus centuries from Lamb, Smith, Shastri, and Azhahadrin, the highlight was not a century but an outstanding innings from Kapil Dev, which saved India from following on.

Going to the middle at 348-6, Kapil Dev stayed with Azhahadrin to the end of the third day with a draw looking the most likely result even though India were still 305 runs behind. The next morning Azhahadrin went in the third over to Hemmings and India still needed 61 runs to avoid the follow-on. Forty minutes later nine wickets were down and 24 runs still needed. Kapil Dev launched into a ferocious do-or-die attack and struck Eddie Hemmings for a record-breaking four consecutive sixes into the building works at the Nursery End. It was just in time, as the last Indian wicket went down off the first ball of the next over. England batted again and set India the impossible target off 472 to win or survive seven hours on a crumbling pitch to save the game, a task that not even Kapil Dev could complete.

78

Unwelcome guest

Wasim Akram b Fernando 78
Pakistan v. Sri Lanka. Colombo, 16 June 2000

Three months after winning a Test series in Pakistan, Sri Lanka were looking forward to celebrating their 100th Test appearance with another victory. Everything seemed to be going according to plan when Pakistan crashed to 176-9 in reply to 273.

But party-pooper Wasim Akram was at the wicket and by carefully shielding his partner, Arshad Khan, for three hours, they were able to add a record 90 for the last wicket before Akram was bowled for 78 from 204 balls. Akram continued to upset his hosts by taking 5-45, including his 400th Test wicket, as Sri Lanka collapsed for 123 in their second innings, and was then in-at-the-death with twenty not out to see Pakistan win by five wickets.

79

Moment of madness

Geoff Boycott run out 79
England v. Pakistan. Hyderabad, 3 and 4 December 1977

England thought they had done well to keep Pakistan down to 275 and at 123-1 in reply looked on-course for a big first innings lead. That was before Abdul Qadir began bowling round the wicket into the bowlers' footmarks and wickets began to fall.

Only Boycott had the right technique to deal with the spin bowler's guile and he seemed to be progressing steadily towards his fifteenth century in Test cricket. Unfortunately, Boycott's tendency to have an occasional moment of madness leading to a run-out, usually of his partner but sometimes of himself, reared its ugly head just when England least expected it and Boycott ran himself out for 79. Then six wickets fell for eighteen runs and England were eventually dismissed for their lowest total in Pakistan, 84 runs behind. Pakistan delayed a declaration until near the end of the fourth day, leaving England with a target of 344 runs in 330 minutes. Boycott and England's captain, Mike Brearley, concentrated on survival rather than risk defeat by going for a victory, and the game ended in a draw with Boycott finally reaching the century he had denied himself in the first innings.

80

Match-winner

Chris Cairns c & b Mullaly 80
New Zealand v. England. The Oval, 21 August 1999

Heavy rain for two days before the game kept the wicket sweating under covers and the ball swung and spun from the start of play. New Zealand did well to reach 236 then saw England crash to 153 with Cairns taking 5-31. With a lead of 83 New Zealand only needed to bat steadily to present England with an insurmountable fourth innings target. But the game swung back in England's favour when six New Zealand wickets fell for 39 runs. Then Cairns came to the middle to smash 80 runs from 94 balls including four sixes and eight fours, which proved to be the match-winning innings. England were finally asked to make 246 to win and made a steady start but their last six wickets fell for just nineteen runs.

81

Accident prone

Nariman Contractor b Greenhough 81
India v. England. Lord's, 18 June 1959

Contractor had established himself in the Indian team and played in 10 Test Matches in India before making his first tour abroad in 1959, although he was still looking for his first Test century. At Lord's he had one of his ribs fractured by Statham but batted on with a runner and his 81 was the top score of the match. When India lost six wickets in their second innings, and were only 82 runs in front, Contractor ignored his injury to go to the wicket again and was eleven not out after the last four wickets fell for 25 runs. It was all in vain as England only lost two wickets before reaching the target of 108 and would go on to win the series 5-0.

Contractor's only other tour abroad was as captain to the West Indies in 1962 but this was cut short when his skull was fractured by a ball from Griffith in a match against Barbados between the Second and Third Tests. After an emergency brain operation Contractor never played Test cricket again.

82

Almost at a standstill

Chris Tavare c Miandad b Imran 82
England v. Pakistan. Lord's, 15 and 16 August 1982.

After playing an important role helping England win the Fifth Test to retain the Ashes in 1981, Tavare had become a regular in the batting line-up at first wicket down and later as an opener.

In the Second Test of the Pakistan tour of England in 1982, England failed to save the follow-on and started their second innings 201 runs behind. It was the first time there had been Sunday play at Lord's and before play was curtailed by rain and bad light in the afternoon, England had slumped to 95-3 losing Randall, Gower and Lamb, with Tavare 24 not out after taking 67 minutes to score his first run. He took another 60 minutes to add to his overnight score and became the first batsman at any level to fail to score during two separate hours in an innings. In his desperate attempt to stave off an innings defeat Tavare took 352 minutes to reach his half-century, the second slowest on record in all first-class cricket. At 3pm he saw England go past the Pakistan total and was eventually out after six hours 47 minutes facing 277 balls for his 82. It was all in vain as Pakistan knocked off the runs required in thirteen overs to record only their second win in England since 1954.

83

A man for a crisis

Eddie Paynter c Richardson b Ironmonger 83
England v. Australia. Brisbane, 13 and 14 February 1933

Eddie Paynter only played in seven Test Matches against Australia but saved England at times of crisis on three separate occasions. As important as the other two were, it was the second rescue act that will always stand out, as it took place during the infamous 'Bodyline' series of 1932/33.

In the Third Test at Adelaide an exchange of angry cablegrams between the MCC and the ABC had almost ended both cricket and diplomatic relations between the two countries. Paynter first showed his mettle on that occasion by going in at 186-5 in England's first innings to make 77 and put them back into the driving seat with a total of 341. But it was during the crucial Fourth Test that Paynter really showed his courage. He had started to suffer from a sore throat during the second day's play, while Australia were batting. When his temperature was found to be 102 and rising, he was taken to Brisbane General Hospital to be diagnosed as suffering from tonsillitis. The next day was a Sunday and he remained in hospital to be visited by his concerned captain, Douglas Jardine. Despite the seriousness of his condition, they reached an agreement that, should England need him at the wicket, Paynter would leave his hospital bed to play his innings. When

276

England's manager, Plum Warner, expressed concern about the risk to the little man's health, Jardine reminded him of the sense of duty shown by English soldiers despite suffering from similar fevers during the Afghan Wars of the nineteenth century and indicated he expected no less. When play resumed on the Monday, Paynter had a wireless at his bedside so that he could keep in touch with England's progress. As they began to lose wickets he wasted no time in struggling out of bed and into his dressing gown and then into a taxi, assisted by team-mate Bill Voce, who was not playing and had been designated as Paynter's personal nursemaid.

Paynter went in to bat soon after tea at 216-6, still 124 runs behind. As he walked slowly to the middle, wearing a wide-brimmed panama hat to protect his fevered brow from the scorching sun and a thick white scarf wrapped around his burning throat, an astonished crowd greeted his unexpected appearance with thunderous applause. Woodfull, the Australian captain, asked him if he would like a runner but Paynter declared it was unnecessary and took guard to face the rampant Australian bowlers, who had just taken the new ball. Despite his weakened condition Paynter held on for 75 minutes, until close of play, with 24 runs to his credit and England now only 69 runs behind. Replacing his white flannels with pyjamas and dressing gown he retired to the hospital for the night.

Next morning, feeling much better after a good night's sleep, Paynter put on 92 runs with Verity for the ninth wicket, occasionally stopping to swallow some medicine for his sore throat and take some tablets, before he was out for 83 and England had edged in front. He even felt well enough to insist on fielding for a couple of hours during Australia's second innings and was back batting again on the sixth day, after a fourth night in hospital, when England won the match by six wickets and regained the Ashes. Paynter himself made the winning hit with a soaring hook shot out of the ground for six.

The third rescue act came five years later after being overlooked for any of the Ashes series matches in 1934 and the tour of Australia in 1936/37. At Lord's he went in at 31-3 and shared a stand of 222 with Hammond, while scoring 99.

84

Prodigious effort

Richard Hadlee c & b Botham 84
New Zealand v. England. Kennington Oval, 15 July 1983

One of the greatest all-rounders in Test cricket, Hadlee's performance in the First Test of the four-match series in England in 1983 was a typical demonstration of the contribution he made to New Zealand cricket throughout his career.

After taking 6-53 in England's first innings he saw New Zealand collapse to 41-5 before going in and making 84 out of a total of 196. It was not enough to prevent an eventual England victory and he would be called upon for another prodigious effort in the final Test (see 92).

85

First time hero

Javed Omar not out 85
Bangladesh v. Zimbabwe. Bulawayo, 21 and 22 April 2001

Bangladesh joined the international cricket fraternity in the year 2000 and their first overseas tour followed in 2001 with two Tests in Zimbabwe. Bangladesh were no match for their hosts and they began their second innings in the First Test exactly 200 runs behind. Wickets fell steadily and Zimbabwe won by an innings despite the heroic defiance at one end by Javed Omar. Omar became the first batsman for over a hundred years to carry his bat undefeated throughout a Test innings on his debut. Pelham Warner was the last batsman to do it, for England in 1898 at Jo'burg, and Omar was only the third to do so since it was first achieved by Jack Barratt playing for Australia at Lord's in 1890. Omar deserved a century for his efforts but at least earned the Player of the Match award, despite his team losing by an innings.

86

New opener does the job

Graeme Fowler c Wasim b Mudassar 86
England v. Pakistan. Headingley, 28 and 29 August 1982

Searching for a reliable opening partner for Chris Tavare after the retirement of Boycott and the temporary banishment of Gooch following his involvement with a rebel tour to South Africa, the England selectors decided to experiment with Derek Randall for the first two Tests of the 1982 series against Pakistan. It was not a success and Randall was dropped back to his preferred place in the lower middle order.

So Graeme Fowler was brought in to make his Test debut. His century partnership with Tavare in England's second innings appeared to have set England up for victory but after Tavare went, the next six wickets fell for 96 runs and England were in danger of not reaching their target of 219. But Fowler was still there and he steered England to a win with three wickets in hand.

87

Qualified success

Basil D'Oliveira not out 87
England v. Australia. Old Trafford, 10 and 11 July 1968

D'Oliveira came to England in the early 1960s to qualify for county cricket with Worcestershire and Test cricket for England, after being prevented from playing first-class cricket in South Africa by the Government's 'apartheid' laws of segregation. Once qualified, he soon showed what a good all-rounder he was and made his debut for England in 1966 against West Indies. Two years later, when the Australians arrived for an Ashes series, D'Oliveira had already played in fourteen Tests, made his first century (against India) and had an average of 41.7, as well as having taken fifteen wickets.

England's hopes of making a good start in their campaign to win back the Ashes were severely damaged when they started their second innings needing 413 runs to win and crashed to 105-5. D'Oliveira playing in his first Test against Australia put up strong resistance and remained unbeaten with 87 but England were 159 short of their target at the end. Australia went on to keep their 1-0 lead right up to the final Test until, thanks to a brilliant 158 from D'Oliveira, England managed to square the series.

For six years D'Oliveira would be a regular in the England team, both at home and abroad, except in South Africa, where the Government's refusal to accept the return of their countryman as an equal member of a touring team meant that they were banned from international cricket until 1992, following the removal of their racial discrimination policy.

88

Pride at stake

Phillip De Freitas c Healy b M. Waugh 88
England v. Australia. Adelaide, 29 and 30 January 1995

England had not won a Test Match in Australia for eight years when their tour began in the winter of 1994/95. They lost the first two Tests of the new series by wide margins, but following the arrival of the Chairman of the selectors, Ray Illingworth, they started to get their act together. They came close to winning the Third Test with Australia desperately hanging on for draw at the end with only three wickets in hand and 104 runs short.

De Freitas had not played in that last match but was brought back for the Fourth Test at Adelaide. There was no chance of regaining the Ashes but pride and reputations were at stake, although England's chances looked slim when several leading players had been forced to return home after injury. Australia took a slender first innings lead of 66 and England began their second innings on the fourth day. England looked to be heading for another humiliating defeat when De Freitas went in at 181-6. Together with Crawley he helped the score advance to

220-6 at close of play. The next morning De Freitas played cautiously for half an hour then launched into a fierce attack and before he was caught at 317-9 he had scored 68 out of England's 108 runs that morning from only 18.5 overs. His total score of 88 had come from only 95 balls. But there was still work to be done as Australia's target was only 263 from 67 overs. The England bowlers rose to the occasion and won the match with 35 balls remaining. Stung by the result, Australia hit back with a massive win in the final Test at Perth, where, for De Freitas, it was a case of 'after the Lord Mayor's Show'.

89

Starting over

Monty Noble c & b Hearne 89
Australia v. England. Old Trafford, 18 and 19 July 1899

This really should be an innings of 149. When Australia were chasing England's first innings total of 372 they slumped to 57-7 on a pitch heavy with overnight dew. Noble had gone in to bat at 14-3 and was still batting when Trumble joined him at the fall of the seventh wicket. They staged a fight back with a stand of 82 and when Iredale joined Noble next they added another 56 for the ninth wicket. It was not enough, and although England would have preferred to bat again and add to their lead rather than ask Australia to follow-on, the Law in operation in

1899 stipulated that if there was a first innings arrears of 120 or more, the follow-on must automatically apply. Australia were 176 behind so back into the field went a reluctant England team with tired bowlers and a wicket that had dried out.

Seeing that Noble was well set after his unbeaten 60, the Australian captain, Darling, made the sensible decision to ask him to go straight back in to open the Australian second innings. It paid off when Noble and Worrall put on 93 for the first wicket and although they lost two wickets, Noble and Trumper were still there at stumps at the end of the second day. The two Australians took the score past the target of 176 to ensure that England would have to bat again and Trumper eventually went at 205. Gregory came and went quickly but first Darling and then Iredale supported Noble while he progressed to 89 after almost five and a half hours at the wicket, including a period of 45 minutes in which he remained scoreless. The victory had been put beyond England and Australia were able to declare 170 runs in front and grab three England wickets before the game ended as a draw, ensuring that Australia retained the Ashes.

Noble's effort, lasting more than eight hours, was one of the greatest rescue acts in Test Match cricket, and all the more remarkable when it is realised that it followed a pair in the previous Test at Leeds, and that he had bowled 28 overs in England's first innings and taken three wickets.

90

Counter-attack

'Jock' Cameron b Nichols 90
South Africa v. England. Lord's, 29 June 1935

It took South Africa 29 years and eighteen Test Matches to win a Test Match in England. And the victory was largely down to the South African wicket-keeper Cameron who changed the course of the match in their first innings. Going in at 98-4 it looked as if South Africa were going to fall well short of a competitive total before Cameron set about the England bowling. Driving and pulling his way to 90 in 105 minutes, Cameron saw South Africa past the 200 mark and eventually beat England by 157 runs.

The other four Tests were all drawn so that South Africa not only won their first Test in England but also won the series.

91

Flying the flag for England

Ken Barrington run out 91
England v. South Africa. Lord's, 24 July 1965

One of England's cricketing heroes of the 1960s, it is no surprise that Ken Barrington features in at least one of the 'Test Match Century' scores. He always gave the impression that he was batting as if his country's future depended upon his ability to stay at the wicket and score runs. Stockily built, he would use a selection of powerful shots only when it seemed safe to do so. From 1959 to 1968 Barrington was the backbone of England's batting. The Australian wicket-keeper Wally Grout, who played against him in four Ashes series, gave the best description, when he said that Barrington 'always seemed to walk to the wicket with a Union Jack trailing behind'.

When a mild heart attack forced Barrington to retire in 1968 he had played in 82 Tests, scored 6,806 runs at an average of 58.67 and made twenty centuries, including at least one on every Test ground in England, and in every Test-playing country of the time. It would have been 21 centuries if it had not been for a brilliant piece of fielding by Colin Bland of South Africa to run him out at Lord's in 1965. Going in at 88-2, Barrington had seen wickets continue to fall at the other end while he steadily progressed to top score of 91 out of 338, giving England a first innings lead of 58.

After his forced retirement three years later, Barrington became a selector and tour manager, but tragically suffered another heart attack while on tour with the England team in West Indies in 1981 and died aged 50.

92

Making a difference

Malcolm Marshall c & b Kapil Dev 92
West Indies v. India. Kanpur, 22 October 1983

On the first day of the First Test of a series of five, West Indies slumped to 157-5 before Dujon joined Greenidge for a partnership of 152. When Dujon was out in the second morning West Indies were still looking for a competitive first innings total and Marshall came in to contribute an exciting and career-best 92 out of a seventh wicket stand of 145 with Greenidge. The final total of 454 proved to be more than enough when in the last hour of the second day Marshall took three wickets for only four runs during an opening spell of extreme pace and ended with four of the five Indian wickets that fell for only 29 runs. Marshall repeated his destruction of the Indian line-up when they followed-on by dismissing both openers in his first three overs and the West Indies cruised to an innings victory with a day to spare.

93

Going to the wire

Dave Nourse not out 93
South Africa v. England. Jo'burg, 4 January 1906

Dave Nourse was South Africa's leading batsman for over twenty years, making 45 consecutive Test Match appearances and he was in the team that achieved its first Test victory.

Plum Warner had brought the first official MCC touring team for a series of five Test Matches in the winter of 1905/06 and when South Africa crashed all out for 91 in reply to England's 184 in the First Test, it looked like being an uneven contest. England made another 190 and South Africa needed 284 runs to win, seemingly an impossible task when Nourse went to the wicket at 105-6. They edged nearer and nearer the target but when the ninth wicket fell they were still 45 short. Nourse was still batting and together with his captain, Percy Sherwell, they finally made it to win by the narrowest margin of one wicket, with Nourse seven runs short of a well-deserved century.

Inspired by this success South Africa went to win the series 4-1 with Nourse scoring 289 runs at an average of 48.1.

94

Another debut at Lord's brings success

Louis Mendis c Fowler b Botham 94
Sri Lanka v. England. Lord's, 28 August 1984

Sri Lanka were invited to play their first Test Match in England in 1984. They made their inaugural appearance at Lord's immediately after England completed their Test series against West Indies, with the home country hoping for a little light relief after losing 5-0 to their earlier visitors.

Sri Lanka won many new supporters after some entertaining batting on the first two days. Mendis became the first Sri Lankan captain to make a century, and after dismissing England for 370, they started their second innings 120 runs in front. At 118-5 at the start of the final day England had hopes of knocking down the remaining five wickets quickly and having a realistic target for the time available. Mendis came in to steady the Sri Lankans and added 138 for the sixth wicket with de Silva to avoid any chance of defeat, finally going six runs short of a well-deserved second century in the match.

95

Steady Eddie

Eddie Hemmings c Marsh b Yardley 95
England v. Australia. Sydney, 6 and 7 January 1983

Going into the final Test 2-1 down, England desperately needed to win to draw the series and retain the Ashes. Because of some bare parches on the pitch, England's spinner Eddie Hemmings was brought into the side in place of fast-medium bowler Pringle. Hemmings had expected that his contribution to England's fight for victory would be with the ball, his Test batting average up to then being only 10.6. He took three important wickets in Australia's first innings and when it came time for England to bat he made a surprising but very useful 29 runs to help England go from 170-7 to 237 although still 77 runs behind. He took another three vital Australian wickets in their second innings but England eventually started the last day one wicket down and needing 452 to win with only six hours available.

In response to his confident batting in the first innings Hemmings had been sent in as nightwatchman for the last twenty minutes and had survived to four not out. Victory became less and less likely as England wickets continued to fall, but at least an honourable draw was possible. Hemmings was 54 not out at lunch and he continued to defy the Australian bowlers and fielders, who by now were resorting to some intensive sledging in an attempt to disturb his concentration. With one hand packed with ice after receiving two nasty blows from fast bowler Lawson, Hemmings kept on scoring, little realising that an examination after the match would reveal that a bone had been broken. While at the wicket he scored 95 runs out of 196, outscoring Lamb, Gower, Randall and Botham and when given out caught at the wicket, Hemmings swore he had never hit it. At least England had saved the game but lost the Ashes.

At the age of 34 Hemmings went on to play another eleven times for England, including making 52 against India in 1990 when aged 41.

96

Last ball draw

Nick Knight run out 96
England v. Zimbabwe. Bulawayo, 22 December 1996

England were asked to score 205 to win from 37 overs. Nick Knight and his captain added 137 for the second wicket to give England a real chance. Negative bowling from Zimbabwe held England back until Knight was run out from the last ball of the match going for the winning run. It was the first Test Match ever to end in a draw with the scores level.

Infuriated by Zimbabwe's tactics, England's coach, David Lloyd, insisted, 'we flippin' murdered 'em!'

97

Stop-start

Sadiq Mohammad c Brearley b Botham 97
Pakistan v. England. Headingley, 29, 30 June and 3 July 1978

Nearly nineteen and a half hours out of the scheduled 30 hours were lost to rain and bad light when England met Pakistan at Leeds in 1978. Play was only possible for less than two hours on the evening of each of the first two days, no play at all was possible on the third day, and only four hours and forty minutes on the fourth day. During this four day period of stop-start action and non-action Sadiq Mohammad went to the wicket on nine separate occasions. He was 34 not out at the end of the first day, 73 not out at the end of the second and third days, and was dismissed just three runs short of his century on the afternoon of the fourth day, after six and a half hours actual batting.

To everyone's relief, rain ended the match early on the afternoon of the final day.

98

Reluctant hero

Harold Larwood c Ironmonger b Lee
England v. Australia. Melbourne, 24 and 25 February 1933

By the time of the start of the Fifth Test in 1932/33 England had won the Ashes. Many expected the England captain, Douglas Jardine, to abandon his 'Bodyline' tactics now that they had served their purpose. No chance. Jardine had no intention of letting Australia off the hook and allowing them the opportunity of recovering some lost pride from an end-of-series victory. He continued with what he preferred to call 'leg-theory' with Larwood as his star bowler, calling on him to bowl 32 eight-ball overs in Australia's first innings.

Much to Larwood's annoyance, Jardine then expected him to bat as England's nightwatchman at the end of the second day after they had gone two wickets down, preferring to hold back Leyland, Wyatt, Paynter and Ames. Despite his somewhat careless approach to his new task, Larwood survived and was five not out at the end of play with Hammond still there on 72. Refreshed by a good night's rest, Larwood restarted his innings in a much more positive manner. He soon began scoring runs all round the wicket and put on 92 runs with Hammond who went on to complete his hundred. Larwood had actually played this sort of innings before, during the MCC tour of 1928/29 when, in the First Test at Brisbane, he had enjoyed a century partnership with Hendren for the eighth wicket while making 70 himself. Now the runs continued to come again and at 98 he looked certain to make his maiden Test century. Then he struck the ball low but straight to the less-than-agile figure of Ironmonger, who surprised everyone – including himself – by holding the catch. Despite having been a figure of hate for the Australian crowds that had packed the grounds during the bad-tempered series, they recognised the quality of Larwood's innings and, sympathising with the disappointment he must have been feeling at missing out on the three figures (which he had richly deserved), sportingly cheered him back into the pavilion.

Thanks to Larwood's efforts, England were able to take a first innings lead and went on to win the match, to the delight of an appreciative captain. But nobody realised that this would be Larwood's last Test Match.

99

Nervous Nineties

Clem Hill c Jones b Barnes 99
Australia v. England. Melbourne, 2 January 1902

The first of many great Australian left-handed batsmen, Clem Hill came to England in 1896 to make his Test Match debut at Lord's at the age of nineteen, but did poorly in the series with only 30 runs from six innings. Sixteen months later, facing England in Australia, he proved his quality by averaging 56.5 for the five-Test series, including his first century. Returning to England in 1899 he played in the first three Tests, averaging 60.2 before being taken ill early in July and taking no further part in what was the first ever five Test series to be played in England.

Hill was fully recovered by the time Archie MacLaren's team arrived in Australia in December 1901 and in the Second Test, after going in at 48-5, became the first player to be dismissed one short of a century in a Test Match. Incredibly, in the next Test he was out twice more in the nineties and became the only batsman to be dismissed for three successive scores in the nineties in Test Matches, 99, 98 and 97. Hill denied that these dismissals were due to any nervousness on his part, and offered three explanations. On 99 he says he had told his partner Duff to be ready for a quick single and therefore rejected the chance to square-cut a short ball to the boundary and tried to steer it to third man, only to be caught in the slips. On 98 at Adelaide, he claimed he was given out, caught by a fielder who had stepped onto the asphalt cycling track perimeter, and in his next innings of 97 he says he misjudged a ball from Jessop that bounced slowly off his pads onto his stumps where the bails remained in place for some seconds before suddenly falling off!

It would be another six months before he finally made it again into three figures. Before his Test career ended in 1912 he was out twice more in the nineties plus making four more centuries, ending with a career average of 39.21 from 49 Tests and touring England on four occasions.

100

Chanceless century

Jack Hobbs b Gregory 100
England v. Australia. Kennington Oval,
16 and 17 August 1926

There have been more that 3,000 Test Match centuries in the past 130 years, but the magic of reaching those three figures remains as strong as the first in 1877.

Jack Hobbs holds the career record of 197 centuries in all forms of first-class cricket, fifteen of them in Test Matches, but none more important than his 100 at the Oval in 1926. Australia came to England that summer having held the Ashes for fourteen years and after four drawn Tests, with neither side in the ascendancy, it was decided that for the first time in England, the final Test would be played to a finish. After fourteen wickets fell on the first day it did not look as if more than the usual three days would be required to reach a result.

Australia were only 22 runs in front when Hobbs and Sutcliffe began England's second innings an hour before stumps were to be drawn on the second day. They resumed their partnership the next morning with 49 runs on the board but few expected them to stay for long. Overnight thunderstorms had drenched the uncovered wicket and once the sun started to shine it would become virtually unplayable until it had dried out. By that time England could have lost most of their wickets and any chance of giving Australia a difficult last innings target. Fortunately, the sky remained overcast for the first hour and Hobbs and Sutcliffe had the chance to play themselves in again on a wicket that gave the bowlers no assistance. When the sun did come out, hot and strong, it immediately caused the spinning ball to fizz and kick viciously, taking lumps of the pitch with it. Arthur Richardson went round the wicket to spin his off-breaks towards middle and leg stumps with three of four short-legs waiting for catches. The two batsmen countered the sharply rising ball by dropping their wrists at the last second as their bats made contact with the ball, denying the fielders any chance of making a catch. *The Times* declared: 'Their artistry in manipulation of the bat was consummate, their judgement infallible, their patience inexhaustible.' During the four previous Tests Hobbs and Sutcliffe had opened all of the England innings with a partnership average of 97.4 and this time they steered England to 161 at lunch with Hobbs 97 not out. Shortly after the interval Hobbs reached his century – his only Test century on his home ground – after three hours and forty-one minutes, without having given a chance. Many consider it to have been the best innings he ever played.

Sutcliffe batted on for another two and a half hours to reach 161 and Australia were finally presented with a target of 415 runs to win, which not even the talents of Woodfull, Bardsley, McCartney, Ponsford, Richardson or Collins had any hope of achieving in a fourth innings played on that rain-affected pitch. The Ashes had finally returned to England and, as Plum Warner wrote in *The Cricketer*, 'This victory means everything to English cricket. Had we been beaten, despondency would have crept over the land.'

0

When is a score not a score?

Don Bradman b Bowes 0
Australia v. England. Melbourne, 30 December 1932

Scorecards list the runs made by each batsman in each innings. They also include the names of the batsmen who have gone to the wicket and failed to score any runs at all. Many such disappointments, featuring some of the greatest batsmen in Test cricket history, have become famous for their dramatic impact. Archie MacLaren became the first opening batsman to be dismissed first ball of a Test Match playing for England against Australia at Melbourne in 1894/95 – a fate suffered by the great Indian opening batsman, Sunil Gavaskar, on no less than three occasions. Then, of course, there was the astonishing 'over from hell' endured by Boycott from the pace bowler Michael Holding at Bridgetown at the start of England's innings against West Indies in 1981. The first ball rose up steeply and Boycott had to glove it away while protecting his face; the second whizzed past his chin; he also missed the third, which hit him on the thigh; the fourth was again short but at least he got some bat on it to steer it safely down into the gully; the fifth whistled past his right ear; and the sixth and final ball sent his off stump spinning twenty yards back to the wicket-keeper, and Boycott returned to the pavilion scoreless.

But one of the most famous of all featured the legendary Donald Bradman.

When Bradman walked to the wicket at Melbourne on 30 December 1932, the first morning of the Second Test, Australia were 67-2. He had missed the First Test through illness but now all Australia was expecting him to put the England bowlers Larwood and Voce to the sword, and demonstrate that not even 'Bodyline' bowling could stop the greatest batsman in the history of cricket from making runs. Even though it was England's third pace bowler Bowes that he had to face first, Bradman was convinced that the first ball would be a bouncer. Determined to take the offensive from the start, Bradman stepped across his wicket ready to hook the ball to leg as Bowes reached the crease and began his delivery. Bradman realised too late that, unsettled by the roar of the crowd as he ran in, Bowes had bowled an innocuous long-hop outside the off-stump, and before the batsman could adjust his stroke his swinging bat dragged the ball back down onto his stumps. Out first ball, when so much had depended on him, Bradman returned to the pavilion with the Australian supporters stunned into silence, while the hitherto cold and unemotional England captain, Douglas Jardine, leapt up and down with a simulated Red Indian war dance.

"

At its best, cricket is the most wonderful entertainment in the world.

Michael Parkinson

"

Acknowledgements

All the statistics for this book have been compiled after reference to *Wisden's Almanacks* 1863–2009, and consultation of the websites cricinfo.com and cricketarchive.com. These sources have been invaluable and my thanks go to their writers and editors.